The Garden Squares of Boston

This book was published in association with

the Center for American Places,

Santa Fe, New Mexico, and Harrisonburg, Virginia

(www.americanplaces.org)

The Garden Squares of Boston

Phebe S. Goodman

University Press of New England

Hanover and London

University Press of New England, 37 Lafayette St., Lebanon, NH 03766
© 2003 by Phebe S. Goodman

All rights reserved

Printed in the United States of America

5 4 3 2 1

Photographs without credits are by the author.

Library of Congress Cataloging-in-Publication Data

Goodman, Phebe S.
    The garden squares of Boston / Phebe S. Goodman—1st ed.
      p.   cm.
    Includes bibliographical references and index.
    ISBN 1–58465–298–5 (cloth : alk. paper)
     1. Garden squares—Massachusetts—Boston—History.
  2. Garden squares—England—London—History. I. Title.
SB466.U65B6728 2004
712'.5'0974461—dc22   2003015321

To Louis

Contents

Conclusion   159

Illustrations

Preface

This book tells the story of transplanting the garden square from London to Boston in the late eighteenth century and the subsequent cultivation in Boston of this urban landscape form. After its first London appearance in 1630, the garden square proved so successful that, during the next 230 years, more than four hundred squares proliferated throughout the city. The inspiration for Boston's garden squares, beginning with Franklin Place in 1793, can be traced to Charles Bulfinch's visit to London in 1785. Although garden squares were laid out in other U.S. cities, Boston's garden squares most closely resemble their London prototypes in both purpose and appearance.

After the town common—an agriculturally based green space created by the settlers of most early New England towns—the garden square is the oldest type of planned landscape in the United States. Never as ubiquitous as the town commons, garden squares were generally confined to the early port towns along the Atlantic seaboard where populations were expanding rapidly. When they first appeared in Philadelphia (1682) and Savannah (1733), they were laid out as part of the original town plan. The earliest planned squares of Boston (Franklin Place in 1793, as has been mentioned), New York City (St. John's Park in 1803), and Baltimore (Mount Vernon Place in 1827) were soon replicated in their respective cities. This multiplicity suggests that garden squares were recognized as an effective urban planning tool for accommodating a growing population.

Although other scholars have published many works about the U.S. public park movement, garden squares, which pre-dated public parks, have received only scant attention. Some contemporary open-space advocates even poked fun at these small token parks. In his 1851 editorial collected in *Rural Essays*, Andrew Jackson Downing, a pioneering U.S. landscape gardener and horticulturist, referred to the squares of New York City as "little door-yards"; he thought them poor substitutes for parks. Yet others, such as Timothy Dwight, president of Yale College from 1795 to 1817, who in the early nineteenth century traveled throughout New England and New York, lamented

Boston's paucity of "public squares," which were "so conducive to health" in Europe. In one of his letters in the collection *Travels in New England and New York*, originally published in 1822, Dwight wrote that if Boston had been laid out on a grid with ten open squares ranging in size from five to ten acres each, "all beautified with selected ornaments," the town would have been the most beautiful in the world.

On the rare occasion when garden squares are mentioned in contemporary landscape histories, they are not differentiated from the town squares that first appeared in many Continental towns and later in many U.S. cities. Physically, both garden and town squares are three-dimensional landscapes with buildings shaping and enclosing an open space that is accessed from abutting streets, and with the sky serving as an outdoor ceiling. But that is where the similarity ends. The historical contexts that gave rise to the two types of squares differ significantly. Consequently, the surrounding building forms are distinct, as is the composition and use of the central open spaces.

The earliest town squares, which pre-dated garden squares by several hundred years, were rarely planned or designed and instead grew organically, often over a period of many years. The buildings in these squares—churches, municipal buildings, and shops—were to be used by the entire community. The squares provided gathering spaces for celebrations or for conducting business. Because these squares often were filled with people, the central spaces at first consisted of hard-packed dirt and later were paved. Although monuments or fountains occasionally were erected to enhance the spaces, vegetation was avoided since it would not have withstood such heavy use.

Town squares—for instance, the grand Piazza San Marco in Venice and the more intimate Piazza SS Annunziata in Florence—usually have been described in terms of their distinguished buildings, with some reference to the historically important events that occurred in these large open spaces. On the other hand, garden squares, with their relatively small gardens and often-unremarkable row houses, have not been the subject of much analysis. A traditional bias among architectural historians toward studying buildings has recently been challenged as more historians realize that buildings should be considered together with their adjacent landscapes. This broadened focus is particularly relevant to garden squares, where the central garden quickly became not only a *raison d'être* of this particular urban form but also its most noteworthy feature.

As has been mentioned, town squares most often developed organically over time in response to community needs, but garden squares were consciously planned by developers who were anxious to maximize profits. As a planned urban landscape form, garden squares were unique for several reasons. Although the streets that ran between the houses and the gardens of the squares were physically connected to the surrounding area, often these streets originally were intended to be private. This meant that the earliest garden squares of London were inward-looking gated enclaves that were not considered part of the public realm. Later, when the streets of the squares were opened to the public, the gardens became a significant—if not well recognized—part of this realm.

Attached row houses turned out to be a very flexible architectural form that developers and builders could manipulate to enclose and shape outdoor spaces of any size or dimension. As a result, squares appeared in many configurations, including crescents, squares, and ovals. For example, when garden squares were inserted into streets— as they often were in Boston's South End—the house lots for the row houses were stepped back gradually to give the squares a gentle curve or bow at the ends. Garden squares always featured a central garden space bounded by streets, an amenity designed to attract builders and residents. These gardens *embraced* the surrounding buildings rather than turning their backs on them as the public parks later did. Finally, in addition to the physical connection between the buildings and the space they enclosed, an equally important social connection existed, for the buildings served as homes for people who had a vested interest in the space.

Developers, in the interest of maximizing the number of houses in a square, laid out narrow lots that could accommodate only attached town houses (row houses) rather than freestanding houses with space on either side. These developers also were stingy in their allotment of a central space on which the houses would eventually front. Since they set aside the smallest amount of space possible to serve as an attraction, the result was usually a relatively modest space intended for use only by the residents, who eventually would seek to embellish and care for the garden. Garden squares usually were distinguished by an appropriate and aesthetically pleasing balance between the height of the surrounding four- or five-story row houses and the size of the central garden.

Garden squares were small neighborhoods, at the outset planned and controlled by the developers and then perpetuated by the residents. As a result they tended to have an air of exclusivity about them—another intended goal. It is important to consider *how* the residents used the gardens because over the years the residents were responsible for maintaining garden squares as a viable urban landscape form. This book will trace the evolution of garden squares—with an emphasis on their gardens—within the context of changing social and economic conditions.

Because all the gardens in the squares were laid out long ago, their preservation has been an ongoing concern of the residents living in the squares. Since 1978 and the founding of the small but influential group called the Alliance for Historic Landscape Preservation, the preservation movement, which previously had focused only on buildings, has begun to champion historic landscapes, which are much more ephemeral. However, just as the preservation treatments recommended for historic buildings are sometimes controversial—asking, for example, whether they should be preserved at all and, if so, to what period—so has the preservation of historic landscapes been the subject of some disagreement. There are critics who feel that a contemporary interpretation of a historic landscape, where little of the original design remains, might be an appropriate treatment. Since most garden squares have their nineteenth-century buildings still intact, this book takes the position that, if at all possible, the gardens should be restored in a manner consistent with their probable nineteenth-century appearance.

Little consensus exists on what to call the type of squares described in this book. Some historians have termed them "residential squares" because they were created as special places for people to live rather than as magnets for civic, religious, or commercial activities. Until recently Londoners always referred to them generically as "squares." Now the term "garden square" has been adopted widely by Londoners, who wish to heighten the public's awareness of the beautiful gardens that traditionally had received attention only from their abutters. This term seems equally appropriate for a discussion of Boston's garden squares, where the gardens also represent the centerpiece of an early urban landscape form in North America.

The development of Boston's garden squares closely parallels that of London's. In both cities the garden square was an early urban planning tool that developers deployed to ensure the success of their project. If an initial square proved financially successful, the property owner—whether in London or Boston—occasionally attempted to attract more buyers by developing additional squares nearby. London grew incrementally according to the whims and designs of private estate owners. Boston, too, grew incrementally, except that in a few areas like the South End the government created a neighborhood. This book will show how the city of Boston, in the pursuit of a broadened residential tax base, took on the ambitious task of adapting a traditionally private landscape form—the garden square—to public ownership. In addition, it will examine Boston's privately developed downtown squares, which had much in common with London's squares.

In creating garden squares, London's estate owners hoped to attract speculative builders to erect well-constructed terrace houses, as they were later called, that would enhance the long-term value of their estates. These residential buildings would then be leased to purchasers, usually for ninety-nine years. In Boston's squares, where the developers also were interested in dividing their property into as many house lots as possible, the ultimate occupants of the houses bought rather than leased the new row houses. The houses of the squares of London and Boston resembled each other quite closely in their uniformity of height and materials and in most often being designed by builders rather than architects. Houses distinguished by a profusion of architectural details, such as those in London's St. James's Square and Boston's Franklin Square, were usually intended for the wealthiest occupants. The narrow terrace houses in London's squares served as part-time, single-family town residences, just as in Boston the early single-family row houses were part-time homes for the more affluent residents of the downtown squares.

In appearance the gardens in such Boston squares as Louisburg and Chester were similar to the London models that may have inspired them. For instance, the signature black iron fence enclosing the garden in the Boston squares closely resembled the iron railings in London's squares. In both cities these fences connoted the exclusivity and privacy sought by both the developers and the residents. Although many of Boston's squares were much smaller than London's, the gardens in the Boston squares, with their characteristic landscape features —grass and an abundance of trees—mirrored those of their English counterparts. For some reason, possibly that rain was so common, London's squares rarely included fountains whereas Boston's cast-iron fountains became showpieces in that city's squares.

To appreciate the traditional components of garden squares one should understand the historical context in which London's garden squares were created as well as the physical features that made them so appealing to those who imported them to several North American cities, including Baltimore, New York, Philadelphia, and Savannah. The discussion of London's squares in the introduction focuses on their development only through the end of the eighteenth century— that is, until Charles Bulfinch transplanted the garden square to Boston shortly after he visited London in 1785. Subsequent chapters, however, touch on nineteenth- and twentieth-century developments in London's garden squares that provide an interesting comparison to their Boston counterparts during these same periods.

Although the primary focus of the discussion is on the gardens, other components of garden squares—their historical context and their buildings—also are considered. In addition to the particular landscape features that define the gardens, several common threads run through the story of Boston's garden squares from their inception to the present: private versus public ownership and access, management and maintenance of the gardens, and preservation treatments. Since these issues are also important to the story of the squares of London, many examples in that city are cited for comparative purposes.

"Downtown Squares," the first chapter, focuses on the influence of Charles Bulfinch, Boston's preeminent architect in the late eighteenth and early nineteenth centuries. Bulfinch is best known for having brought neoclassical architecture to New England. Less well known is his role in transplanting the garden square directly from London to Boston.

"South End Squares," the second chapter, traces the planning process adopted by the city to increase its tax base and reduce its rapidly growing municipal debt by keeping middle-class residents from moving out of Boston toward emerging communities, such as Jamaica Plain, at the city's edges. This process, which was an outgrowth of Bulfinch's visionary South End plan, relied on garden squares as a tool for creating exclusive residential enclaves similar to the three privately developed downtown squares.

The third chapter, "Evolution and Preservation," traces the evolution of the South End squares from the Panic of 1873 to the present. The current challenge for residents of the South End squares is to forge a productive relationship with the city for the purpose of clarifying and prioritizing maintenance and preservation concerns and to advocate for the allocation of more municipal resources to the restoration of these historic landscapes.

The conclusion provides a summary of the themes presented in the book and a comparative analysis of the challenges currently facing the stewards of the garden squares in Boston and London. In the absence of well-informed decisions regarding appropriate preservation treatments, the future of these historic garden squares will be in jeopardy. The people of Boston can ill afford to lose these unique urban landscapes to inattention or inappropriate design schemes.

A Note to the Reader

Although this book is based on years of research and professional landscape preservation work, the text is presented without explanatory endnotes in order to facilitate its appeal to a general readership. Sources should be self-evident in the text. Scholars who desire specific reference citations can write to me, care of University Press of New England. The bibliography at the end of the book indicates my primary and secondary sources of information.

Garden squares can be found in residential neighborhoods where a visitor least expects to find them. I recently discovered Belmont Square (now called Brophy Park) in East Boston. Created in 1833 by the East Boston Company, it was designed to attract residents when that part of Boston was first being developed. Nine beautiful Greek Revival brick bowfronts with wonderful Egyptian Revival granite and iron fences still front on a garden that essentially retains its nineteenth-century design. I hope this book will enable you to see garden squares in a more critical way. I also would enjoy hearing about any garden squares you happen upon—wherever they might be.

Acknowledgments

I would like to express my gratitude to three longtime residents of the South End who not only read sections of my manuscript and offered valuable insights but also shared many of their personal treasures with me. Richard Card, the first president of the South End Historical Society, showed me his fascinating collection of letters written by members of the Everett family between 1851 and 1859. John Neale, current historian of the South End Historical Society, unearthed many of his old city plans for me. David Hocker, who has restored his magnificent house in Chester Square, made available his rare stereographs of the South End squares. Without access to these materials, much of my depiction of the South End during the mid–nineteenth century would have been more speculative and more limited.

I would also like to thank Henry Lee, Beacon Hill resident and longtime leader of the Friends of the Public Garden and Common, Boston's preeminent park advocacy group, for reading the chapter on downtown squares and offering many helpful comments. I am grateful to two people across the Atlantic who responded to my continued barrage of questions about London's garden squares: Holly Smith, editor and publisher of *Garden Square News*, and Drew Bennellick, landscape architect for English Heritage. Without their help it would have been more difficult for me to understand what was happening with London's squares today.

In the case of the South End, which has been so sparsely documented in books, one picture is worth many, many words. But historical pictures of the South End are also relatively rare. To those archivists in the picture libraries of many of Boston's venerable institutions who directed me to the existing photographs, I express my gratitude. The archivists in other cities who supplied me with photographs also deserve thanks for their efforts. Enabling readers to find

Boston's squares was a major goal of this book, and I am pleased that the two maps designed by Bill Kuttner will greatly simplify the task of visiting the squares.

Jane Lewin read the entire manuscript in an early stage, and I am grateful for her encouragement and many insightful comments. Input from peer reviewers Gina Crandell, adjunct professor in the Rhode Island School of Design's Department of Landscape Architecture, and William A. Mann, professor in the College of Environment Design at the University of Georgia, helped focus my thinking and writing. George F. Thompson, president of the Center for American Places, believed in the project and found the right publishing home for my book. The editors at University Press of New England lavished care on the project. Finally, I would like to thank Phyllis Andersen for introducing me to the South End squares many years ago and my entire family for having the patience to listen to me talk about squares for the past ten years.

Newtonville, Massachusetts   P.S.G.

The Garden Squares of Boston

INTRODUCTION

From London to North America

$\mathscr{T}$HE STORY OF THE CREATION of London's garden squares is not about perceiving a need to create small gardens for the general populace but, rather, about creating exclusive enclaves of attached houses fronting on private gardens. Sixteenth- and early-seventeenth-century London, which was rapidly transforming from a medieval town into a major port, did not suffer for want of green open spaces. Just outside the city walls were many heaths and common lands that Londoners could use for recreational purposes, particularly sports. By 1625, the popular Moorfields to the north of the city was laid out as a large pleasure garden, with a formal design that included *allées* of trees and walkways to encourage more sedate activities such as promenading. During the first half of the seventeenth century, large tracts of land were opened to the public. Nearly a century earlier, King Henry VIII had appropriated this land from the monasteries and then, for the most part, had used it for his personal hunting grounds. Although these royal parks—St. James's Park, Green Park, Hyde Park, and Kensington Gardens—had become more accessible to London's citizenry, they still remained Crown property.

After the first quarter of the seventeenth century, the descendants of the noblemen who had received large parcels of land from Henry VIII began to search for a suitable real estate development model that would be profitable and would also enable them to retain long-term control of their property. Lincoln's Inn Fields was London's first garden square, having started out as a large, green meadow with walks adjacent to Lincoln's Inn, one of London's Inns of Court. In 1629, William Newton, a speculative builder, obtained from King Charles I —who could not resist the prospect of increased revenue from the property—a license to build thirty-two houses on the edge of the Fields. Although the members of Lincoln's Inn opposed the plan, Newton prevailed, and by 1641 most of the attached houses on the west side of the square, farthest from the Inn, and all of those on the south side had been erected. In 1657, as buildings were planned for the final two sides of the square, a formal agreement was signed ensuring that the seven acres of open space would remain green. The garden was laid out with gravel walks and grass plats surrounded by a low wooden fence.

Covent Garden Piazza, commissioned by the fourth Duke of Bedford in 1630 as a speculative building venture, is widely considered by Londoners as the progenitor of all the squares, even though it never contained a garden. It is generally agreed that this square—designed by Inigo Jones, who had made many trips to Italy—was inspired by two Continental squares, the Place des Vosges in Paris and the Piazza Grande (a church square surrounded by arcaded shops) at Livorno, Italy. Jones, surveyor to King Charles I, was the first architect to successfully introduce into England the Palladian style, which was characterized by excellent proportion, symmetry, and frequent use of the classical orders. He designed a Tuscan-style church, St. Paul's, flanked by two smaller buildings for one side of the square. Arcaded residences for the nobility occupied two sides, and the gardens of Bedford House, the duke's home, formed the fourth side. During its early years Covent Garden, with its central open space that could be used for strolling or riding, was a fashionable town address for upper-class residents, most of whom also had country homes. However, beginning in 1671 when the fifth Duke of Bedford was permitted to have a daily vegetable market in the central space, Covent Garden was gradually transformed into a commercial town square and lost its status as a prestigious residential square.

In the aftermath of the Great Fire of 1666, both landlords and speculative builders were provided with an unprecedented opportunity to profit from the acute housing shortage. Just before the fire, a few noblemen, inspired by the success of Lincoln's Inn Fields and Covent Garden, had begun planning their own garden squares. The goal of the estate owners was simply to introduce, for their own financial advantage, amenities that had previously been lacking in the city. These new attractions included town houses that would serve as seasonal residences for aristocrats when they were not enjoying their country estates; a central garden that functioned as an elegant site for promenading as well as an attractive ornament when viewed from the surrounding houses; and the convenience of a nearby church and market. Gated streets and fenced-in gardens were the ultimate symbols of the privacy and exclusivity intended by the landowners and sought after by the residents.

In planning Bloomsbury Square in 1665, the fourth Earl of Southampton, whose estate passed to the Duke of Bedford only two years

later at the earl's death, used a form of speculation that was eventually adopted by almost all the estate owners. The significant components of this land-speculation scheme were as follows. A master-builder would sign a building agreement with the landlord. During the first year or two, while the builder was erecting one or more buildings that he would immediately offer for sale, he would pay a small "peppercorn" rent to the landlord. If the builder found a purchaser before the end of this "peppercorn" period, his initial investment would be minimal, and the purchaser would sign a ninety-nine-year lease with the landlord. The purchaser was then in a position to dictate many of the final details of his new house, and the landowner could sacrifice immediate profits in favor of enhancing the future value of his estate.

In the case of St. James's Square, the Crown granted land to Lord St. Albans in 1665 with the understanding that he would establish an appropriately fashionable district, given its proximity to St. James's Palace and the royal park of the same name. Although St. Albans had initially envisaged a square with as few as three or four mansions for noblemen on each side, the increased demand for housing created by the 1666 fire prompted him to sell twenty-three smaller plots around the square either to aristocratic friends or to building speculators.

Bloomsbury Square by Sutton Nichols, ca. 1725. Courtesy of the Museum of London.

This engraving shows the simple design of Bloomsbury Square's garden, with grass plats enclosed by wooden fences, sixty years after the Earl of Southampton created one of London's earliest squares in front of his mansion. In keeping with the view from his house open, he sacrificed potential income from a fourth side of terrace houses.

St. James's Square by Sutton
Nichols, ca. 1725.
Courtesy of the Museum of
London.

This engraving of St. James's
Square shows the center of the
square shortly after the trustees
received permission from the
Crown to "clean, adorn and
beautify" it. Designed by
Charles Bridgeman, the basin—
150 feet in diameter, with a
central *jet d'eau*—is surrounded
by an iron fence with obelisk-
shaped lampposts.

Despite St. Albans's insistence on a uniform height of four stories,
including dormers, for the new, attached dwellings, the widths and
styles of their façades varied. As part of this fashionable new residential enclave, which included a house he had built for himself,
St. Albans also arranged for the construction of several streets, a large
poultry and meat market not far from the square, and a church,
Christopher Wren's St. James's, Piccadilly. Because the large central
space of St. James's Square initially was covered with dirt (for parking
carriages) and gravel (for promenading), the primary attraction for the
numerous elite residents must have been the opportunity to live in
close proximity to their social peers, at least for part of the year. During its first hundred years the square was home to no fewer than ten
prime ministers, several lord chancellors and foreign secretaries, and
an assortment of other prominent people.

It was during the Georgian period (1714 to 1811) that London
emerged as a world trading power, with growing mercantile wealth
and a burgeoning middle class. Driven by the high cost of building
lots and the need to fit as many houses as possible onto a street, speculative builders used only narrow-fronted attached houses built of
brick and placed on relatively deep lots. Usually some space was left

in back of the houses for small courtyards as well as coach-houses and stables served by a secondary street or alley. Both the stables and the alleys on which they fronted were called "mews." Several successive building acts, culminating in the Building Act of 1774 (which, for fear of fire, imposed limitations on the use of exposed woodwork), resulted in uniform houses with barely any external wooden ornamentation. According to British architectural historian John Summerson, the proliferation of pattern books, while bringing the classical idiom to master-builders and craftsmen alike, was also responsible for contributing to what many Londoners felt was "the inexpressible monotony of the typical London street."

Until the middle of the eighteenth century the Palladian style of architecture dominated the taste of the day, and its popularity was reinforced by two publications, Colin Campbell's *Vitruvius Britannicus*, and the first English translation of Palladio's *Quattro Libri*. During the second half of the century the neoclassical style introduced by architect Robert Adam (1728–1792) exerted a strong influence on London's architecture. Adam's neoclassical ornamentation, consisting of delicate swags, slim pilasters, and narrow moldings, revolutionized the building trade, and after 1775 there were few buildings with interiors that did not show traces of his innovative style. Stucco, an inexpensive material for simulating stone façades, was also useful in creating the kind of ornamentation on building exteriors that reflected the new interiors, and it rapidly became Adam's signature.

The 1770s and 1780s represented the boom decades for the construction of Georgian town houses. The palace-style façade, recommended by Palladian pattern books and distinguished by pilasters and a pediment, was introduced at the center of a row of terrace houses and added a note of elegance to the otherwise simple buildings. This architectural enhancement, which had become quite popular, was used in Bedford Square (built between 1775 and 1783) and translated into increased sales for the speculative builders. Bedford Square was also the first square in London to have uniform houses on all four of its sides. Most squares, both earlier and later, could not achieve this architectural uniformity because they were subject to the vagaries of speculative development, which meant that the houses on each side were often built at different times, and by different builders, depending on what the market could support.

Despite their narrow dimensions, terrace houses provided sufficient space for the active social lives of the middle and upper classes of Georgian society. Isaac Ware, author of *A Complete Body of Architecture* (1756), described the typical town house as having five stories, including a basement and attic, with two large rooms as well as a small "closet" on each floor that could serve as a dressing room or servant's bedroom. In addition to a formal dining and drawing room, town houses also included a parlor, a kitchen, bedrooms, and servants' rooms—all within a building whose average dimensions were often no more than twenty feet wide by forty feet deep. The principal story (usually on the first floor above the ground floor) contained the reception rooms and had the highest ceilings and tallest windows. The spacious dwellings in St. James's Square, where the frontages ranged from forty-four feet to fifty-four feet, could more easily accommodate their residents' active social season. Summerson cites as an example of one of these more extravagant buildings, 20 St. James's Square, which was designed by Robert Adam for Sir W. Williams Wynn in 1772, and he notes that Adam's houses were built for continual entertaining in drawing rooms, anterooms, and dining rooms.

The estate owners who laid out London's first squares during the seventeenth century must have sensed that some open space would be a welcome contrast to the density of the surrounding town houses, yet they did not necessarily envisage these spaces as gardens. Originally intended both for parking carriages and for promenading, these spaces often became dumping grounds. As the social parade began to play an increasingly important role in the life of the Georgian aristocrat, the residents of the squares began to clamor for more elegant stages for their socializing—gardens that would provide an impressive focal point for the relatively undistinguished and confining dwellings. As the residents became self-conscious about the neglected appearance of their common front yards, they began to petition the government for permission to assess rates on the garden's abutters to pay for improvements. The St. James's Square Act of 1726, the first of several such acts, granted permission to the residents "to clean, adorn, and beautify" the square.

Although London had approximately fifteen garden squares by the end of the eighteenth century, architectural historians have not focused on the gardens even though they played an important role in these squares. Like the buildings in the squares, which reflected to various degrees the contemporary architectural styles of freestanding houses translated to narrow terrace houses, the gardens tended to emulate the landscape styles of England's expansive country estates, albeit on a very small scale. Even though landscapes are ephemeral—rarely surviving even fifty years—and landscape styles seem to go in and out of fashion, it is possible to trace the evolution of many of these gardens by using prints of the period, particularly those of Sutton Nichols in the first quarter of the eighteenth century. These prints show formal layouts with straight paths, geometric grass plats, and the ubiquitous fences—all reflecting the formal French and Dutch styles that were then in fashion.

By the end of the eighteenth century a marked shift in landscape styles had occurred both on England's country estates and in London's royal parks, as landscape designers William Kent, Lancelot "Capability" Brown, and Humphry Repton introduced such natural-looking features as groups of trees, small shrubs, and grass. When elements of this new pastoral style began to appear in the garden squares, the gardens were often described as *rus in urbe* (a bit of "countryside in the city"). Not everyone was enamored of this new style. James Stuart, in his *Critical Observations on the Buildings and Improvements of London* (1771), ridicules the *rus in urbe* concept that recently had become so popular, observing that "A garden in a street is not less absurd than a street in a garden."

Two eighteenth-century prints of Bloomsbury Square illustrate the very simple design of its garden. In 1725 the garden, surrounded by wood fencing, has grass plats and straight paths. By 1787 a large greensward has a pathway around its perimeter just inside an iron fence. By the time Bedford Square was laid out in 1775, the estate owner knew that the respectable upper-middle-class residents he was trying to attract (as opposed to the more aristocratic ones sought by St. Albans for St. James's Square) had become increasingly interested in having enhanced gardens. Bedford Square was the first square

View of Bloomsbury Square, ca. 1787. Courtesy of the Museum of London.

Fifty years after the earlier engraving, the garden in Bloomsbury Square is still primarily grass, but it is now enclosed by an iron railing with gas lamps attached. Although only two women are strolling within the garden, the cobblestone carriageway is bustling with people, animals, and carriages.

St. James's Square, Acker-
man's Repository, ca. 1809.
Courtesy of the Museum of
London.

In this engraving of St. James's
Square, a statue of King William III on a horse is placed on
a pedestal in the center of a
basin. The surrounding fence
has been changed from an octa-
gon to a circle. It was not until
1818 that John Nash moved the
fence to its present position,
thereby greatly increasing the
area of the garden.

where the landlord not only envisaged a central garden right from the
start but also paid the builders to construct it. Shortly after the square
was laid out, its garden reflected the naturalistic English style with its
traditional elements of trees, shrubs, and grass. All that was missing
was a water feature. The use of water, which was prevalent on the
large country estates, was not practical in these small garden spaces,
although St. James's Square contained a large basin of water for much
of the eighteenth century and well into the nineteenth. The garden
in Bedford Square was enclosed by an iron fence, a feature that was
more attractive and transparent than the heavier brick or wood fences
of the earlier squares. "Iron railings," as they were commonly called,
with locked gates for which only the residents had keys ultimately
became a signature feature of all garden squares. Yet despite the locked
gardens and gated streets, garden squares were never completely protected from occasional public disturbances.

The landlord and his leaseholders shared the responsibility for keeping the garden and perimeter roads in good condition. The leases
granted by the Duke of Bedford contained covenants according to
which the lessees were to pay a share of the expenses for repairing the
roads, the lighting, and the garden's iron railings. Although the residents were also obligated to bear all the expenses of the enclosed garden, they often turned to the landlord whenever any major work
needed to be done. Occasionally the estate itself would initiate improvements. During the first half of the nineteenth century Bedford

Square, with its naturalistic English-style garden, was one of the best addresses in Bloomsbury, if not the very best.

As this overview of the evolution of London's garden squares during the seventeenth and eighteenth centuries makes clear, the social and economic forces that led to the creation of these squares remained unchanged for 170 years. The landowner, serving as chief planner, sought long-term financial gain from respectable upper- or middle-class residents, who paid a premium to live in an exclusive neighborhood. Given the narrow dimensions of the terrace houses and the small size of the gardens, the use of ornamental architectural details and elaborate landscape elements was bound to be limited. Yet the houses and gardens in the squares, which were designed to be modest in scale, evolved gradually over the years, reflecting the dominant styles of the day.

During the seventeenth century the Palladian style of architecture prevailed, along with very simple gardens consisting of grass plats and a few trees. By the first half of the eighteenth century the enclosed gardens, used only by residents for promenading and viewing, had become quite formal, with straight paths, borders of trees and shrubs, and occasionally some type of central feature, such as a fountain or statue. By the end of the eighteenth century, as Adam's neoclassical style of architecture eclipsed the earlier Palladian style, the gardens in the squares began to take on a more naturalistic appearance, emulating the newer and more naturalistic styles of Kent, Brown, and Repton. Throughout the entire period from 1630 to 1800, the gardens were surrounded by some form of enclosure that symbolized the privacy and exclusivity sought by both the estate owners and the residents.

Philadelphia, Savannah, New York City, and Baltimore

Although garden squares had proved to be very popular in London, five North American cities, including Boston, embraced this landscape form as an early planning tool. Each of these East Coast cities—Philadelphia, Savannah, Boston, New York, and Baltimore—ultimately became thriving mercantile ports just like London, but the role garden squares played in each city did not always replicate the London model. The garden squares of Philadelphia and Savannah, which appeared much earlier than those in Boston, served as focal points in the original grid plans of those two cities. Even though London's squares were not part of an overall city plan, they almost certainly provided the inspiration for the squares of Philadelphia and Savannah. But unlike London's squares, the squares of Philadelphia and Savannah were never intended to be speculative real estate ventures. Instead they were planned as public amenities or common lands for the entire community.

The garden squares of New York and Baltimore, contemporaneous with Boston's nineteenth-century squares, were much more like those of London and Boston because they were laid out rather cautiously—one at a time—so that the developer could get a sense of whether the investment would be successful. Those who sought financial gain through the creation of garden squares must have been familiar with London's garden squares. Just as in Boston, New York had both private and public squares. The gardens in all of Baltimore's squares were built on land given to the city by private developers, who were confident that the value of their abutting property would increase once the garden space was improved. As background for this book's discussion of Boston's garden squares, it is instructive to examine briefly the garden squares in the four other East Coast cities where their popularity—even today—further underscores the historical significance of this early landscape form.

Even though Bulfinch figuratively took the garden square directly from London to Boston, he would have been familiar with Philadelphia's squares. As the first large North American city to be laid out in a grid pattern, Philadelphia included a major innovation that was to serve the city well for three centuries—five large public squares, four of which were intended as recreational green spaces. In 1682, William Penn (1644–1718) directed his surveyor, Captain Thomas Holme, to lay out the city of Philadelphia in a grid between the Delaware and Schuylkill rivers. In the center was a ten-acre square, named Center Square, which was set aside for such public buildings as a market house, meeting house, and school house. Penn also specified that there be an eight-acre square in each quadrant of the city "to be for the like uses as the Moorfields in London." The inspiration for this plan may have been a combination of Lincoln's Inn Fields and the grid plans advanced in London in the wake of the Great Fire of 1666. Penn's visionary "green country town," where every house was surrounded by gardens, orchards, or fields, rapidly evolved into a mercantile town that eventually bore little resemblance to Penn's idyllic vision.

Philadelphia had become an important port well before the American Revolution. As an increasing number of three-story row houses were constructed to accommodate the growing population of merchants, the original large city blocks were cut up so that more streets with dwellings could be constructed. As early as 1720, *The South East Prospect of the City of Philadelphia*, a painting by Peter

Cooper, shows red-brick row houses similar in style to London's terraces. By the middle of the nineteenth century the city's five large, open spaces seemed diminished by the incessant repetition of the grid pattern with streets and alleys lined with narrow row houses.

Although Penn had assumed that his city would develop first along each waterfront and then expand toward the center, residential development occurred exclusively at the eastern edge along the Delaware River. While Center Square functioned as a thriving marketplace twice a week, the other four "green" squares served as burial grounds and pastures for cattle until their designation in 1825 as Washington, Franklin, Logan, and Rittenhouse squares. Beginning with the eastern squares (that is, Franklin and Washington squares), the city soon began to enhance the spaces with fencing, trees, and grass to make the neighborhoods more attractive. By 1831 the garden in Washington Square had been laid out with large, circular plots planted with many varieties of trees. Frances Trollope, visiting the city from England in the early 1830s, noted in her book *Domestic Manners of the Americans* that Philadelphia was "beautiful but built with extreme and almost wearisome regularity." Trollope commented that Washington

"This Plan of the City of Philadelphia" by John Hills, 1796.
The Library Company of Philadelphia.

Center Square and the city's four other squares laid out equidistant from the main square are evident in this plan of Philadelphia. Development is not clustered at the center, as Penn had anticipated, but rather spread along the Delaware River between the northeast and southeast squares, identified as "Burying Grounds" on the plan.

This lithograph shows the
remarkable transformation of
the square from a burial ground
in 1796 to a beautiful garden
square, the centerpiece of
which is a fountain. Installed
in 1838, this fountain featured
forty jets of water and was
surrounded by an ornamental
iron railing.

Square, surrounded by houses on three sides, was "the nearest approach to a London square that is to be found in Philadelphia." She
described the garden with its numerous trees and comfortable seats as
a "very agreeable retreat."

By 1839 the garden in Franklin Square, or Northeast Square as it
originally was called, had been improved with all the traditional furnishings of garden squares—trees, grass, and a grand fountain
enclosed by a decorative iron railing. By 1842, Logan Square had
trees, grass, and walks, and it was enclosed by a wooden fence. Finally
Rittenhouse Square, or Southwest Square, was improved in 1852
with an iron fence, trees, grass, and walkways. The neighborhood
around this square, filled with fine row houses and mansions overlooking the garden, soon became the most fancy residential section of
Philadelphia.

Savannah, founded by English general James Oglethorpe (1696–1785),
was laid out in 1733 along the Savannah River according to a plan of
four "wards." Each of these ten-acre wards contained a one-acre
open "square" bordered by streets. Oglethorpe gave separate names
to each ward and square, thereby adding importance to the open
spaces. Two more wards with squares were added to the plan within
the next two years. A total of four "trust" lots were reserved for pub-

lic buildings on the east and west sides of the squares, while on the other two sides a total of four "tythings" of ten lots each were granted to the new colonists for their individual homes. Each lot, measuring sixty feet by ninety feet, allowed for a small garden space in addition to a one-story dwelling.

Although Ogelthorpe's plan may have been inspired, in part, by European military designs that reflected the colony's purpose as a buffer between South Carolina and Spanish Florida, English garden squares were also a possible model. Some of the Georgia trustees had not only participated in the development of London's early squares, they had even lived in St. James's and Hanover squares. Oglethorpe himself would have known about Penn's plan for Philadelphia, with its four "green" squares and a larger central market square. By scaling down the size of his open spaces to one acre and limiting the number of house lots around them, Oglethorpe ensured that the city would have no difficulty in replicating the wards as the population grew. Following Eli Whitney's invention of the cotton gin in 1793, the city of Savannah rapidly became a prosperous world port, with the result

Stouf's 1818 Plan of the City of Savannah.
Courtesy of the Georgia Historical Society.

This plan shows fifteen squares, all within close proximity. The gardens—which not long before had been embellished with trees, paths, and fountains—were the focal points of the surrounding neighborhoods. The space in the upper left portion of the plan became Crawford Square and Ward in the 1840s.

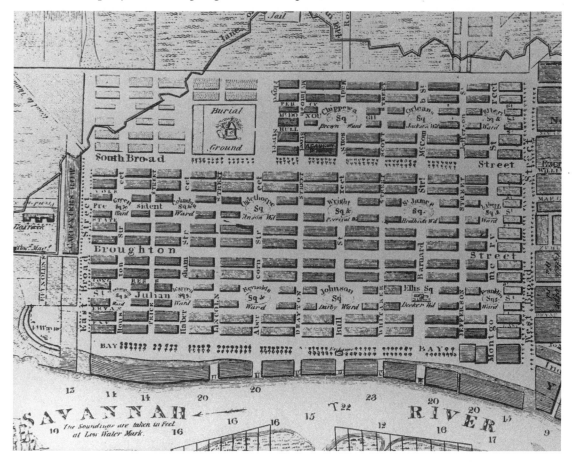

that by the mid-nineteenth century an additional eighteen wards with squares had been created.

Savannah's squares were never used for military purposes but instead served as marketplaces, locations for wells and water pumps, and even small pastures for cattle. By the early nineteenth century, the squares were becoming centers of social life. The city council resolved to improve and enhance its then-thirteen squares by enclosing them with painted white cedar posts connected by chains, planting them with trees and Bermuda grass, and installing paved footpaths. In his classic history of Savannah, *Savannah Revisited*, Mills Lane documents the comments of several visitors to the city in the 1830s. In 1833, Sara Hathaway of New York described each of the many gardens as "enclosed with a railing, laid out with walks and planted with shade trees and rustic seats arranged in them all about." In 1839, James Silk Buckingham of England described the squares with their "grass plats and trees" as "peculiarly pleasing" and noted that they offered "the most rural appearance imaginable." By the mid-nineteenth century Savannah's overall "green" appearance was a reflection of the relatively large number of garden squares (twenty-four) within a two-square-mile area.

Since the port of Savannah never had to accommodate the dense populations that flocked to the northern mercantile cities of Philadelphia, New York, Baltimore, and Boston, the city's speculative builders were not under pressure to squeeze in as many house lots as possible around the squares. As a result the ubiquitous row houses characteristic of the garden squares in the northern cities were relatively uncommon. Instead, the merchants who profited significantly from Savannah's single-product economy—cotton—tended to build large (by contemporary standards) mansions.

The squares of Philadelphia and Savannah did share several common features, however, that distinguished them from their London prototypes. The open squares in both cities were important features of an overall city grid plan proposed by the first English settlers, and they were intended to be public gathering spaces. Because they were laid out in multiples, each square, except for Philadelphia's Center Square, was designed to serve as a garden square for its surrounding neighborhood. As dwellings were built around the squares of each city, the municipal government, rather than the house owners, bore the responsibility for enhancing and caring for the open spaces. The garden squares served the open-space needs of their respective cities until the growing populations demanded more. Philadelphia's Fairmount Park, the largest municipal park in the country, was established in 1865; and Savannah's Forsyth Park, first privately owned, was given to the city in 1851.

The garden squares in New York City were not laid out as part of an early city plan but were instead isolated efforts to provide attractive green spaces for affluent residents. At the end of the American Revolution, the population of what was soon to become the country's largest city was clustered at the southern tip of Manhattan, where the streets were narrow and winding. By that time Bowling Green, which had begun during the seventeenth and early eighteenth centuries as both a parade ground and cattle market, had evolved into a half-acre garden serving as the focal point for the city's most fashionable neighborhood. As the city prospered and rapidly became the economic capital of the country, encroaching commercial buildings gradually began to push its residential population northward.

When city commissioners superimposed a grid plan on Manhattan in 1811, they were more interested in enhancing the city's potential for real estate development than in providing amenities for a growing population. Since Manhattan had the advantage of being surrounded by water, they designated very few new open spaces to serve as small

Bowling Green in 1797.
From *Valentine's Manual*, n.d.
Museum of the City of New York.

The garden of this residential square is enclosed by a fence brought from England in 1771. The oldest public park in New York, the garden was established in 1733 "for the recreation and delight of the inhabitants of the city." A statue of King George III, installed in 1770, was destroyed during the Revolution.

parks or squares. Tompkins and Stuyvesant squares were new garden squares that fit into this grid plan. The gardens of both squares, which were originally parts of private estates donated to the city, were subsequently enhanced by the city and were always open to the public. Union and Madison squares eventually were created in locations where the preexisting swath of Broadway, which cut across the grid, made the future construction of buildings impractical. Samuel Ruggles (1800–1881), who was responsible for creating the private Gramercy Park, also advocated for the enhancement of the gardens in both Union and Madison squares through individual assessments even though he was a property owner in both squares.

New York had two private garden squares that were similar to London's private squares, St. John's Park and Gramercy Park. By 1803, when Trinity Church planned St. John's Park (sometimes referred to as "Hudson Square" because of its location in lower Manhattan near the Hudson River) for residential development, the people involved would have been familiar with the financial success and beauty of London's many squares. When Samuel Ruggles laid out Gramercy Park in 1831, the houses and garden in St. John's Park, which were then being developed, may have served as a local prototype, for there is no record of his having visited England prior to 1846. The gardens in both squares bore the distinguishing features of London's garden squares: iron fences, trees, and grass. By the middle of the nineteenth century even the gardens in New York's public squares were furnished with iron fences, fountains, trees, and grass.

All of New York's squares, whether public or private, were lined with row houses that were similar to London's terrace houses. As a result of the great concentration of wealth and the presence of a large and prosperous middle class, nineteenth-century New York row houses were significantly larger and grander than their counterparts in Philadelphia or Boston. By the 1840s, the use of brownstone—a symbol of wealth and architectural sophistication—for the ornamental trim and façades of New York's buildings was much more prevalent than in any other city. In Union Square (where the three-and-a-half-acre park opened in 1831) and Madison Square (where the six-acre park opened in 1847), the city's furnishing of the gardens sparked construction of palatial brownstone-fronted row houses and occasionally mansions. By mid-century both squares were fashionable residential neighborhoods, but by the turn of the century they had become commercial districts. Before Central Park was opened to the public in 1859, the gardens in New York's squares were the only green spaces available to serve the needs of a population approaching eight hundred thousand.

· · ·

Because the port city of Baltimore grew rapidly as a mercantile center, it is not surprising that developers chose to create several garden squares. In 1790, Baltimore was the fourth largest city in the nation after New York, Philadelphia, and Boston. Starting in the 1820s, with a shift in its economy from maritime trade to manufacturing, additional housing was needed for the prosperous merchants. Since Baltimore's 1823 grid plan did not allow for any public open spaces, private developers had to receive special permission from the city to lay out Mount Vernon Place and other garden squares less than two miles from the city's downtown area. These speculative real estate ventures resulted in public gardens that enhanced the value of the abutting property that still belonged to the developers.

In 1827, Mount Vernon Place—four small garden squares in the shape of a Greek cross—was laid out on property donated to the city by the heirs of John Eager Howard. More than ten years earlier Howard had donated the land on which the Washington Monument in Baltimore, located at the convergence of the squares, was erected beginning in 1815. Because of the relatively remote location of Mount Vernon Place (about a mile to the north of the harbor area), construction of most of the houses did not begin until the 1840s. The four small garden spaces were soon surrounded by beautiful Greek Revival town houses occupied by the city's most socially prominent citizens. Until fences were installed in 1850, the spaces were dirt rectangles where boys played games. In the 1880s, the fences were removed, and the gardens were landscaped with walkways, plots of grass, and fountains.

In 1839, the Canby brothers gave the city two-and-a-half acres of land—later part of Franklin Square—for a small park in West Baltimore. The city agreed to fence in the park as soon as all the buildings around it had been constructed. As was the case in most squares, the houses in Franklin Square were not built simultaneously but rather one side of the square at a time. The first brick row houses were built on the west side in 1850. In 1851 an impressive row called Waverly Terrace, which was distinguished by a highly ornamented cast-iron balcony extending the entire length of its façade, was erected on the east side. In 1852, after all the buildings had been completed, the city installed a fence and fountain and planted the entire garden, which soon became a popular spot for passive recreation.

Ultimately four additional garden squares—Union, Lafayette and Perkins squares, and Harlem Park—were created in West Baltimore between 1847 and 1872. As in Mount Vernon Place and Franklin Square, private developers donated to the city land for the gardens in these squares. The public gardens of these later squares, with their walkways, grass, trees, fountains, and iron fences, eventually were surrounded on each side by three-story, three-bay Italianate row houses, which had been built on a speculative basis. Although the row houses in these squares were not as architecturally distinguished as those in Franklin Square, all of the squares became desirable neighborhoods for prospering middle-class residents who wished to live relatively close to the downtown area. Concurrently with the creation of West Baltimore's five garden squares, three more—Madison, Johnson, and Collington squares—were developed in East Baltimore between 1853 and 1880. The garden-square model obviously had proved to be effective in attracting residents to each newly developing area of the city, even after the opening of the five-hundred-acre Druid Hill Park in 1860.

In New York and Baltimore, whenever one square was laid out, others seemed to follow within a relatively short period. Considering the benefits that garden squares could provide to their developers—they were both profitable and easily adapted to the existing street systems —it is surprising that these squares appeared so infrequently in other U.S. cities. The social and economic conditions of the East Coast cities in which garden squares were either created or enhanced during the nineteenth century had much in common with the conditions that had existed in London in the mid-seventeenth century when garden squares first appeared. The use of the garden-square form was limited to prosperous mercantile cities that sought to provide housing for increasing numbers of affluent and middle-class citizens.

The creation of a group of squares required willingness on the part of a developer to forego, for the purpose of enhancing his property, using the land that would remain open. Although in New York and Baltimore the initial impetus usually came from the private sector, in most cases—except for St. John's Park and Gramercy Park—the gardens were intended to be open to the public. As this book will show, Boston's South End was an unusual example in which the city played the role of developer. In order to be successful the public garden squares in Boston, New York, and Baltimore required a delicate balance of public and private support that other mercantile cities were not able to achieve.

Boston's Garden Squares

The two-hundred-year history of Boston's garden squares begins with Bulfinch's creation of Franklin Place in 1793. As the designer of Franklin Place, which was undertaken as a speculative real estate venture in downtown Boston, Bulfinch created a small crescent of elegant, attached dwellings and a group of four detached double houses that fronted on a small garden space. The major difference between Franklin Place and the London squares was that in downtown Boston, space was at such a premium that Bulfinch allocated only a very small area for his garden square and, in fact, was unable to create a second, matching crescent. Franklin Place served as the model for Boston's two other privately developed squares—Louisburg Square (1826) and Pemberton Square (1835)—which were also created downtown, in an area where there was a perceived need to provide housing for prosperous businessmen.

A comparison of these downtown squares to those of London shows that the financial motives of their developers were quite similar, as were the types of buildings used to shape their central spaces. Like the squares of London, Boston's downtown squares were connected to nearby streets, but only in Louisburg Square were the streets within the square privately owned. For want of space, as in London, the more economical row houses had gradually replaced Boston's freestanding mansions. And while the row houses in Louisburg and Pemberton squares were relatively plain in comparison to Bulfinch's crescent houses in Franklin Place, they still managed to attract affluent buyers, many of whom appreciated the convenient in-town location. To a certain extent the gardens did serve to enhance the real estate values of the houses in the squares, as their planners had intended. Although the gardens in downtown Boston were small, they still required effort on the part of the residents, who were solely responsible for their care. Despite their small size, they were enjoyed not only by the residents, who could look out on them, but also by the public at large, which was attracted to these tranquil patches of greenery in an increasingly dense and bustling city.

Several years after he created Franklin Place, Charles Bulfinch—by then the city's chief administrator—displayed great vision by laying out the five-acre Columbia Square as the centerpiece of Boston's new South End district. This square, which was ultimately divided and given two names—Blackstone and Franklin (as distinct from Franklin Place) squares—became the model for a series of six additional garden squares that the city created in the South End during the mid-nineteenth century.

Although the financial success of the downtown garden squares might not have been quite as great as the city perceived it to be (Bulfinch went bankrupt, and the house lots in Louisburg and Pemberton squares did not sell quickly), the city still believed that a major investment in new squares would prove to be financially rewarding. The South End squares represented the city government's only attempt to plan an entire district in much the same way that London's estate owners had developed their estates. The city was fairly timid in the amount of space it chose to allocate when it laid out its six new squares. By inserting the squares into an existing street plan, the city created squares that were of necessity long and narrow. Except for Chester Square, where the street was exceptionally wide, this constraint resulted in the South End squares being quite similar in size to the squares downtown, where overall space limitations rather than street width had dictated the size of the squares.

In several of the South End squares the row houses were much more grand than the houses in Louisburg and Pemberton squares. The presence of many more architectural enhancements reflected Victorian taste at the middle of the nineteenth century. Although the landscape features of all the gardens in the South End squares were very similar to those of the downtown squares, three of the gardens in the South End squares—those in Blackstone, Franklin, and Chester squares—were much larger and more like those in the squares of London. The major difference between the gardens in the South End and downtown squares was not so much how they looked as in how they were cared for. In the downtown squares the new residents embellished and cared for the gardens right from the beginning. In the South End, on the other hand, the city not only planned the gardens as an incentive to attract speculators before the abutting lots were sold, but it also committed itself to furnishing and even maintaining the gardens before most of the houses were built. Once residents moved into their new houses, they were often dissatisfied with the simple treatment of grass and trees that the city had provided and sought to further enhance the gardens with flowers. In the case of Chester Square, the residents even decided to pay for their own gardener. Although the gardens were owned by the city, once the residents began to take a proprietary interest, they locked the gates and essentially privatized some of the gardens.

During the last quarter of the nineteenth century the South End was eclipsed as a fashionable residential district, and the squares no longer kept their elite status. As the middle classes moved out, single-family row houses were converted into lodging houses, and the city lost interest in caring for the gardens. A fortunate result of this precipitous decline was that, because the city chose not to allocate many financial resources to the district, the South End became frozen in time. Although the row houses deteriorated, they were not demolished. The gardens in the squares were also neglected, but no one coveted the spaces for any other use. In 1913, the city, acknowledging that the gardens needed to be upgraded, commissioned a comprehensive survey of its squares. Although the survey provided valuable documentation, it resulted in few improvements.

In the late 1950s, when the South End became a target for urban renewal, the residents became more interested in preventing the destruction of the neighborhood's physical fabric. Gradually disparate groups began to coalesce, and the city finally agreed to tear down only a quarter of the housing and to support rehabilitation of the rest. Although rehabilitation of the gardens in the squares was not a priority of urban renewal, the residents who remained in the squares, along with the newcomers who moved in, began to take an interest in improving them. Economic revival soon gave rise to increased advocacy efforts for enhancements. In response to community concerns, the city was able to allocate public funding to restore some of the gardens. Fortuitously, some major private linkage funds associated with the development of a nearby medical complex were earmarked for Blackstone, Franklin, and Worcester squares for a ten-year period. When this commitment expired in 2000, the city had no plans for providing consistent public funding for their upkeep. Two years later, the tenuous public/private partnerships that had emerged for the purpose of maintaining and restoring the gardens were not as effective as they could have been because both partners still perceived and treated each of the South End's eight squares as a separate neighborhood.

Over the years, whether in the privately owned Louisburg Square, the publicly owned South End squares, or any of London's squares, maintaining and preserving the gardens has required significant investments of volunteer time, energy, and money. The next step toward improving the maintenance and preservation of these squares is to make their stories better known.

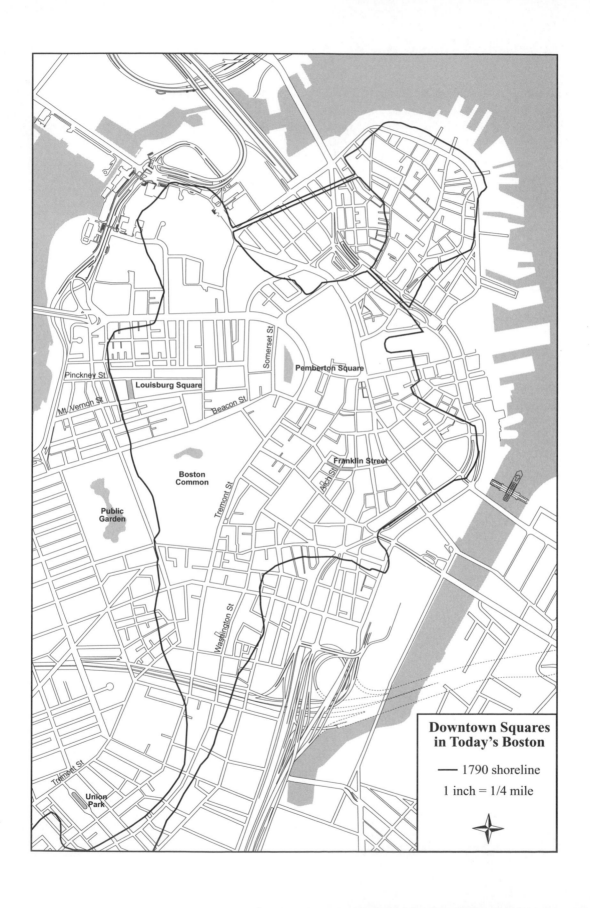

Pinckney St

Louisburg Square

Mt. Vernon St

Beacon St

Somerset St

Pemberton Square

Boston
Common

Franklin Street

Arch St

Tremont St

Public
Garden

Washington St

Tremont St

Union
Park

**Downtown Squares
in Today's Boston**

—— 1790 shoreline

1 inch = 1/4 mile

Chapter One

DOWNTOWN SQUARES

𝒪F BOSTON'S THREE privately developed garden squares, all of which were located close to the original center of the city, two are now lost. Only Louisburg Square survives. Franklin Place, designed and built by Bulfinch in 1793, was located so close to Boston's burgeoning business district that it was only a matter of time before the encroaching businesses would sweep it away. All that remains of it today is the wide, crescent-shaped swath of Franklin Street, lined with retail stores and some office buildings. Pemberton Square, a residential enclave laid out in 1835 on a slope in the heart of the downtown area, suffered the same fate. Today Pemberton Square is a paved, crescent-shaped open space accessible only to pedestrians and sandwiched between the Suffolk County Court House and a long, curved office building.

Louisburg Square, laid out in 1826, is tucked into the middle of the affluent Beacon Hill neighborhood behind the Bulfinch-designed State House, where it is barely visible today from even a block away. This square has become a well-known Boston icon. Its nineteenth-century town houses, façades largely intact, appear frozen in time. All those who visit the square's tiny green oasis nestled between the town houses are struck by the lushness of its trees, shrubs, and well-manicured lawn as well as the exclusive atmosphere conveyed by the original tall, iron fence and adjoining cobblestone streets. Except for the very small size of its garden, which discourages access and yet encourages viewing by the abutters, Louisburg Square is similar to London's garden squares, both physically and historically.

Boston's three downtown squares were created by wealthy individuals eager to profit from the perceived need for attractive residential areas near the center of a rapidly expanding city. As was the case in London during the middle of the seventeenth century, these individuals were interested in limiting the size of house lots in order to maximize their financial return. But because the private estates in London were much larger than any urban holdings that Boston's developers could amass, London's squares tended to be significantly larger than those in Boston. Nevertheless, the same principles applied in both cities: squeeze as many dwellings as possible into a location convenient to the business district, placing the homes around a central garden that would provide a sense of space and "nature" to a layout that would otherwise seem very dense. In London, new houses that were physically joined to one another on narrow lots came to be called terraces—perhaps after the well-known Adelphi Terrace, a row of houses built by the Adam brothers in 1772 on a terrace overlooking the Thames River. In Boston, such buildings were commonly referred to as row houses. The term "town house" was often used in both cities to connote an attached dwelling that was located in a fashionable urban neighborhood.

Historical Context

"Boston" was the name given to the Shawmut Peninsula by the group of English Puritans who settled there in 1630. In 1743 the town was the largest port in British North America, with a population of around sixteen thousand inhabitants. By 1760, with its population having leveled off, Boston fell to third position, behind Philadelphia and New York City. Although Boston remained a bustling seaport after the Revolutionary War, it still had space available for further development within the confines of the Shawmut Peninsula.

The peninsula contained a prominent ridge, the Trimountain, marked by three peaks—Mount Vernon to the west, Beacon Hill in the center, and Pemberton Hill (also known as Cotton Hill) to the east. At its southern extremity a narrow neck of land connected the peninsula to the mainland. During the seventeenth and early eighteenth centuries the town, with its irregular layout of streets, expanded gradually in a manner typical of mercantile cities: streets followed the growth of trade and were not planned in advance. Until the late eighteenth century the largely undeveloped Trimountain continued to loom over the inhabitants of Boston. In 1799, however, the Mount Vernon Proprietors, a syndicate of wealthy Bostonians, cut down Mount Vernon to create more space suitable for residential development. This was one of many occasions when the city's topography would be altered substantially to accommodate a growing population, and garden squares would often figure prominently in the real estate developments resulting from these earth-moving projects.

In the early nineteenth century, while some of Boston's wealthy citizens were busy altering the geography of the city, others were more concerned about severing their cultural and emotional ties to their mother country. Although they were committed to establishing a unique identity, Bostonians often ended up creating new institutions inspired by English originals. As many of the merchants and sea captains who had amassed fortunes after the Revolution became preoccupied with building new homes for themselves and public buildings for their fellow citizens, they sought a style that would combine good taste and a lack of ostentation. The Federal style of architecture that Bulfinch introduced turned out to be consistent with the Puritan values and aspirations of this newly rich group because it rejected the earlier, heavier Palladian style, which had come from Georgian England, in favor of more delicate and attenuated lines and proportions.

It is generally accepted that Charles Bulfinch (1763–1844) created the Federal style by adapting Robert Adam's neoclassical style, which had been fashionable in London when Bulfinch made his Grand Tour from 1785 to 1787. Upon his return from Europe, Bulfinch both created and defined the architectural taste of the day by incorporating a modified neoclassical style into designs for his many wealthy clients. He is best known for his designs of private mansions in Boston, the most famous being the three Harrison Gray Otis houses, all still standing, and for his many public buildings, including the State House and the reconstructed Faneuil Hall. Yet he was also the architect for several of Boston's earliest row-house developments, all now lost: Franklin Place, which is discussed below in detail; Park Row, a group of four attached houses on Park Street opposite the Boston Common; and the Colonnade, nineteen row houses on Tremont Street, also facing the Common. The fact that all of these houses fronted on gardens demonstrated Bulfinch's sophisticated understanding of the important role that such spaces could play in enhancing the livability, and therefore the desirability, of downtown locations.

Franklin Place

Bulfinch's Grand Tour was influential in stimulating his appreciation of "the beauties of nature and art." He spent much of his time abroad visiting friends in London and seeing some celebrated places in that area. Although his correspondence from England did not refer to his impressions of well-known local landscapes, a letter from Marseilles extolled the virtues of "one or more public walks shaded with trees and kept in constant repair." A close study of Bulfinch's Franklin Place, Boston's first garden square, reveals many features, particularly the use of attached houses surrounding a central garden, that were

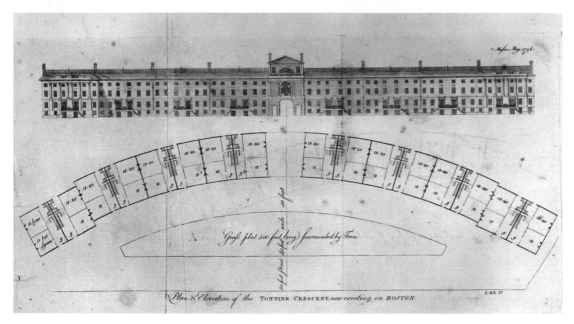

Plan and Elevation of the Tontine Crescent now erecting in Boston.

This engraving appeared in *Massachusetts Magazine* in February 1794, when only half of the buildings had been completed. The description accompanying the plan explains that the name "Franklin Place," in honor of Benjamin Franklin, has been chosen to "dignify this scene of improvement."

innovations for Boston but can be traced to the garden squares Bulfinch would have seen in England.

Bulfinch's intent was to establish a new and fashionable residential district south of the central business district in what previously had been an undeveloped area of fields and marshlands. Although the focal point of this neighborhood was to be a residential garden square called Franklin Place in honor of Benjamin Franklin, Bulfinch's vision included more than just dwellings and a garden. By creating the Boston Theatre (1793) at the northeast end of the square and Holy Cross Church (1800) directly opposite the theatre at the southeast end, Bulfinch was introducing additional amenities for the residents, just as St. Albans had done in London's St. James's Square. Bulfinch's theatre and Catholic church, both financed by private subscriptions, were innovations for Puritan Boston, which until December 1793 had banned theatrical performances and for almost two hundred years had often demonstrated religious intolerance.

Bulfinch's creation of sixteen houses joined in a crescent shape on the south side of Franklin Place—often referred to as the Tontine Crescent—was also a new concept for Boston, which until the Revolution still had enough space in most locations to accommodate single dwellings with small gardens. As land values began to rise, however, many newer dwellings began to be built with their narrow ends to the street and their entrances on the side. In building a long row of attached houses, Bulfinch was taking a chance that wealthy individuals would not mind living in relatively cramped quarters. He would have known that most wealthy Londoners who lived in garden squares also had country estates, and perhaps he believed that Bostonians who might be interested in living in Franklin Place would have summer homes elsewhere with large gardens.

An advertisement in the Boston weekly *Columbian Centinel* for the week of July 6, 1793, announced "that a plan is proposed for building a number of convenient and elegant HOUSES, in a central situation, on a scheme of tontine association." Although the plan generated some interest, fewer than half the project's shares had been sold when construction began later that month. Despite lagging sales, a subsequent advertisement indicated that construction was continuing in the hope that "the work already done will give a favorable opinion of the solidity and elegance of the Houses, and induce gentlemen to subscribe." The fact that more than a year passed before all the shares were sold may have meant that Bulfinch had misjudged Bostonians' appetite for a new style of in-town living.

Although Bulfinch's use of the crescent shape for his new development cannot be traced to any specific London examples, he may have been inspired by the beautiful crescent shapes of the Circus (begun in 1754) and the Royal Crescent (begun in 1767), both of which he would have seen during his visit to Bath. However, both the relatively large scale and the heavy Palladian style of these buildings would not have been compatible with the Federal neoclassical style he had already begun to introduce to Boston. Considering Bulfinch's attraction to the neoclassical style of Robert Adam, it is possible that he was inspired by a purported Adam design (which was never built) for two semicircles of houses facing each other, with a garden space in the center, at the end of Portland Place in London. Bulfinch had originally planned a matching crescent for the north side of Franklin Place but ultimately had to settle for a linear configuration of four double houses because he was not able to acquire sufficient land for another crescent.

Instead of basing their real estate venture on the traditional English leasehold system, in which buyers purchased houses already built by speculative builders and then signed leases with the estate owner, Bulfinch and his partners used the popular European tontine plan as their economic model. In a tontine system participants bought shares, with the fund going to the subscribers who survived after a specified time. Unfortunately, Bulfinch's lack of experience in real estate development prevented the financial success of the project and ultimately led to his bankruptcy. During 1793 and 1794, the *Columbian Centinel* carried several advertisements seeking subscribers to the crescent.

In designing the crescent's central building, Bulfinch adapted Robert Adam's neoclassical design for the façade of the Royal Society of Arts building in London, just as he had for the Joseph Coolidge house

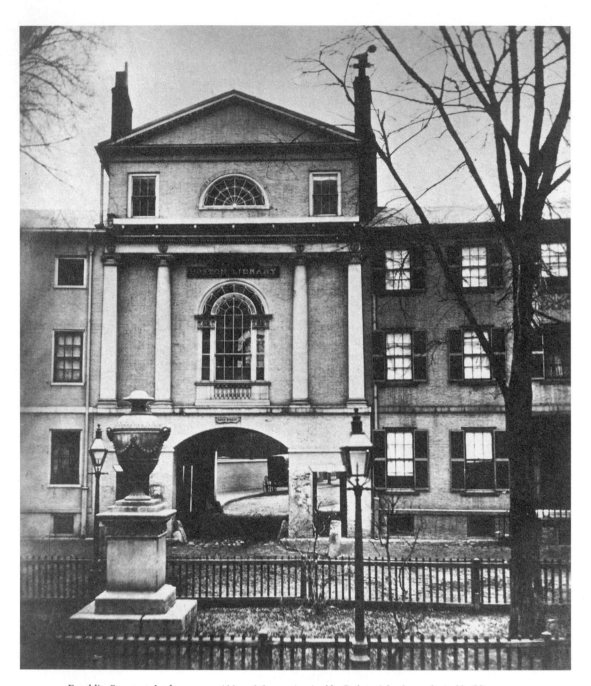

Franklin Street at Arch
Street, 1853.
Courtesy of The Bostonian Society/
Old State House.

Although he was inspired by Robert Adam's neoclassical buildings,
Bulfinch cleverly replaced what could have been an elaborate entrance
to the central pavilion with a simple archway that permitted Arch Street
to enter Franklin Place. The urn, purchased by Bulfinch in Bath, England, pays homage to Benjamin Franklin, who died in 1790.

in Boston several years earlier. This pavilion, however, included an arched passageway (through which Arch Street ran south to Summer Street) with a large room above it as well as an attic story. Bulfinch and his partners soon realized that it might be difficult to find buyers for the pavilion's two rooms, which may have been unsuitable for residences. According to the 1794 deed, they presented the "upper apartment or room in the center building in Franklin Place in Boston called the Crescent" to the Massachusetts Historical Society, which had been founded in 1791 as the first institution devoted primarily to collecting and publishing material concerned with American history. In 1796, they gave the large room behind the neoclassical Palladian window to the Boston Library Society, which had been founded in 1792, and which later merged with the more successful Boston Athenaeum, founded in 1807. Both Bulfinch and his partner, Charles Vaughan, were among the first trustees of the Boston Library Society. Thus, when prompted to provide free space in his new building, Bulfinch chose as the recipients two new cultural organizations that were modeled after private British institutions of the period and that also provided a certain cachet to Franklin Place.

Bulfinch completed the crescent in 1794. It was four hundred feet in length and included sixteen attached brick houses whose identical doorways were spaced two to a porch. The structure contained all of the defining neoclassical elements of the new Federal style: attenuated pilasters on the central pavilion and two end pavilions that projected forward several feet, swag panels, and delicate fanlights and lunettes. Although the four-story houses (including an attic and basement) were one story lower than most London terraces, they were in other respects quite similar to their London counterparts. Each floor consisted of two large rooms, which *Massachusetts Magazine* described as "spacious and lofty," with a hallway on one side containing both the main and the service stairways. The houses were equipped with all of the latest conveniences: pumps, rainwater cisterns, and stables that could be accessed by a back alley. This alley with its stables was intended as an important amenity for the residents and was similar to the mews behind London's squares.

At the end of 1794, Bulfinch began work on the four detached double houses directly across from the crescent, which served to complete the square. The two center units, which included tiny fenced-in front gardens, were much larger than the pairs at the ends, which were angled slightly to keep the street openings as wide as possible. Whereas swag panels embellished the buildings in the crescent, recessed brick arches—a hallmark of Bulfinch's style—distinguished the new double houses. Despite their higher selling prices, these houses were more popular than the smaller crescent row

houses. Federal society clearly preferred the larger size and greater lot frontages that these dwellings offered.

The exteriors of the Franklin Place dwellings were brick—a relatively new innovation for Boston's residential buildings of the period. The brick was painted gray to simulate stone, and the architectural details, carved from wood, were painted white. Bulfinch's use of paint on brick was inspired by the introduction of painted stucco over brick in London as a result of the Building Act of 1774, which limited the use of wood for building façades. The use of stucco rather than stone—a more expensive material—soon became a popular method for relieving the monotony of endless stretches of brick houses that were being constructed. The Adam brothers used stucco on two houses that they designed in St. James's Square. In Bedford Square, the palace-style façades of the middle building on each side of the square (which included Ionic pilasters) also were made of stucco. Bulfinch used paint innovatively as a very simple and inexpensive treatment that gave his new buildings a more refined appearance, one that would have appealed to the elite of Federal society he was trying to attract. In 1794, *Massachusetts Magazine*, commenting on Bulfinch's Tontine Crescent, which was still under construction, called its style "the most approved of modern elegance."

Boston's first garden square, Franklin Place, was unusual not only for its shape and the fact that it was the city's first row-house complex but also because it was designed by a talented architect. The designs of the houses in most of London's squares have generally been attributed to speculative builders rather than architects. The terrace houses of Bedford Square in Bloomsbury, for example, a square that was considered by many to be perfect because all its sides matched, were unremarkable and had almost no architectural embellishments except for the palace-style façade on each side. The seventeenth-century houses in St. James's Square were originally uniform and not particularly distinguished, but in the eighteenth century several famous architects modified their façades. However, the impressive buildings of both the King's Circus and the Royal Crescent in Bath—which, as mentioned earlier, may have been the inspiration for the Franklin Place crescent—had been designed by the well-known architects John Wood the Elder and his son, John Wood the Younger, respectively.

In the garden squares that Bulfinch might have seen in London, the houses—while important in shaping the squares and serving as residences—were ultimately of less interest to both the developers and prospective residents than the garden spaces, which distinguished these prestigious enclaves and made them especially attractive. In the case of Franklin Place, however, the unique configuration of the houses dominated the square. Also, the architectural style of the dwellings in Franklin Place was so distinguished that it surpassed what Bulfinch would have seen in most of the terraces in London's garden squares. Although Bulfinch's original plan included a small garden, this garden was never mentioned as a selling point in the advertisements for the crescent houses—perhaps because it was so tiny.

The narrow, semi-oval garden in Franklin Place, which measured only 40 feet wide at its center and about 280 feet in length, was significantly smaller than the gardens in London's larger squares. Yet the great expanse of buildings forming a crescent, which was echoed in the shape of the garden and its adjoining streets—each 30 feet wide —suggested the importance of this imposing space despite its small size. Regarding the garden, *Massachusetts Magazine* wrote in 1794:

> The figure of a crescent has been adopted, as, independent of the beauty of the curve, it afforded an opportunity of introducing a green or grass plat surrounded by trees, which will contribute to the ornament of the buildings, and be useful in promoting a change and circulation of air.

A significant difference between Franklin Place and London's private squares, where gated streets allowed entry only by residents, was that access to the garden was not restricted. Although the deeds to the Franklin Place houses stipulated that the small garden was provided "for the accommodation, convenience and beauty" of the residents in the square, visitors to the Massachusetts Historical Society and

Boston Library Society as well as theatre-goers and people attending church would have enjoyed viewing the garden. Shortly after the crescent's completion, the newly widened Arch Street was extended through the center archway, and other connecting streets were opened to the south and east. The addition of these new streets reflected the growth of the downtown business area immediately surrounding Franklin Place—a trend that would eventually doom the square.

Even before Franklin Place was completed, Thomas Pemberton, a historian and active member of the Massachusetts Historical Society, appreciated the significance of Bulfinch's inclusion of a garden. Writing in 1794, he described the grass plat as being surrounded by trees and enclosed by posts and chains, and he noted, "This is supposed to serve the purposes of health by purifying the air, and at the same time it adds a natural ornament to artificial beauty." In the same account Pemberton also captured Bulfinch's public-spirited intentions: "We may anticipate that when complete, it will be a favorite part of the town, and in some degree its boast."

Writing as he did in 1794, Pemberton did not mention the large urn that had yet to be placed in the garden—a memorial to Benjamin Franklin (who had died in 1790) that Bulfinch installed, possibly as soon as all of the houses in Franklin Place were completed in 1795. This urn, which occupied a prominent position on a pedestal in the garden directly opposite the archway, was significant because of its connection to Robert Adam. It was almost identical to a Robert Adam design originally executed by the Parsons family, which dominated trade in the Bath stone garden vases that were extremely popular in the eighteenth century, both in England and abroad. Such vases were usually placed in large landscapes, along with fountains and statues. Anticipating that he would eventually find an appropriate use for them, Bulfinch might have purchased the urn and pedestal in Bath as a souvenir of his Grand Tour. In the late 1850s, when Franklin Place was demolished, the urn and pedestal were moved to the site of Bulfinch's grave in Mount Auburn Cemetery in Cambridge, where they remain today.

Although Bulfinch had to sell his interest in the entire project before it was completed, by 1798 all of the residences in Franklin Place had been sold and were occupied by the families of prominent businessmen and men of letters. In this respect, Franklin Place was successful; it achieved the social stature that Bulfinch had envisioned —the exclusivity that was such an important feature of London's garden squares. At least half of the original owners were among Boston's most successful merchants, men whose businesses were located on the wharves. Franklin Place's "convenient" and "central" location had clearly proved to be an asset. At 3 Franklin Place lived James

As seen through the dark drapery framing *The Tea Party* and echoing the archway between the two rooms, the furnishings and the elegantly attired guests reflect Sargent's grand vision of high-style entertainment in Franklin Place. This scene may even reflect a social occasion in the artist's own home.

Perkins, merchant and principal donor to the Boston Athenaeum's first building, who in 1822 donated his Pearl Street estate to serve as the Athenaeum's fourth home. Among the men of letters were William Tudor, Jr., founder of the periodicals *Monthly Anthology* and the *North American Review*, and his literary associate Dr. John S. J. Gardiner, rector of Trinity Church. The only two female property owners were Abigail Howard, one of six women who were founders of the Boston Library Society, and Elizabeth Amory.

The type of social life that residents of Franklin Place would have participated in was suggested by two paintings now in Boston's Museum of Fine Arts: *The Dinner Party,* circa 1821, and *The Tea Party,* circa 1824, both by Henry Sargent (1770–1845). Sargent was a popular painter of the period who had studied in London under Benjamin West. These pictures probably represent actual parties that took place in the artist's house at 10 Franklin Place, which was part of the crescent. Bulfinch's original plan and elevation of the Tontine Crescent provides an interesting basis for comparing some of the crescent's architectural features to the layout of the rooms depicted in both paintings. Since each floor contained two rooms measuring approximately eighteen feet by eighteen feet, the two rooms depicted in *The Tea Party* must have been two adjoining parlors, most likely on the second floor above the first-floor dining room. The graceful archway connecting the two rooms in the picture is a neoclassical architectural detail that Bulfinch used to relate the interior of the house to the neoclassical Palladian window on the crescent's central building.

The frontage of each house in the crescent measured only twenty-seven feet (much like the frontage of the average London terrace house), which allowed only two rooms per floor, one behind the other. This long, narrow configuration did not inhibit the scale of entertaining that took place, in part because the "lofty" ceilings must have made the rooms seem larger than they actually were. Bulfinch's drawing of the crescent's elevation suggests that the windows of both the first and second floors were of the same height. The interiors of the rooms shown in the two paintings are consistent with this plan. In most London terraces of the period, however, the second-floor parlor windows were usually taller than the windows on the first floor (known as the ground-floor level).

The furnishings depicted in Sargent's paintings represent contemporary high-style Boston interiors, which in most respects were similar to their London counterparts. Although the dining room in *The Dinner Party* is quite masculine, with mahogany furniture and large portraits appropriate to the gathering of gentlemen, the two parlors or drawing rooms depicted in *The Tea Party* are lighter in feeling, more feminine, and ornamented with many French and Italian decorative objects. The women, adorned with the latest and most expensive fashions of the day—column-like Empire gowns with accompanying shawls—look as if they might be dressed for a tea party in a London town house.

Because of its central, downtown location, Franklin Place was relatively short-lived, lasting only sixty-three years. After about thirty years, at a time when the Mount Vernon Proprietors were developing an exclusive residential neighborhood on Mount Vernon just to the west of Beacon Hill and were beginning to lure affluent residents farther from the central business district, middle-class residents began to replace the wealthy occupants of Franklin Place. Franklin Place's single-family dwellings were soon converted into boarding houses. The new residents were less interested in the overall appearance of the neighborhood than their predecessors had been. In photographs of the square taken in the 1850s, shortly before its demise, the garden appears overcrowded with small shrubs planted randomly among the trees, which had finally reached a height suitable for the scale of the space. An inappropriate wood picket fence has replaced the original iron posts and chains.

In early 1858, the city, having already taken the crescent dwellings "for the public convenience," offered the Boston Library Society $12,000 for its room. In 1833, the Massachusetts Historical Society had moved to a building on Tremont Street next to the burial ground of King's Chapel, because it had outgrown its quarters over the arch and also because the members were afraid of fire, which could prove much more devastating to a row of attached buildings. Soon all of the square's buildings were razed and replaced by large granite warehouses. All that remained of the garden was a single elm tree and three empty circular pits where other trees had stood in the middle of the wide, crescent-shaped curve of Franklin Street, formerly called Franklin Place. If the square had remained an enclave of affluent individuals, they might have been in a better financial position to resist the march of commerce. With the exodus of these residents there was no one left to protect the little garden that Bulfinch had placed in the middle of a crescent-shaped public street that still had the potential to be a great urban space.

In 1859, *Ballou's Pictorial Drawing-Room Companion* presented two engravings of "Franklin Street," one as it appeared in 1858, before the dwellings were torn down, and one as it appeared on January 1, 1859, when stores and warehouses had replaced the houses. The accompanying article, although admitting the inevitability of the triumph of commercial over residential interests in this central area of Boston, recommends that readers consider moving to the South End, which in 1859 was still regarded as quite fashionable. As has been noted, Franklin Place lasted only sixty-three years—a relatively brief period for such an architecturally distinguished enclave. Yet its influence was felt in Boston's Louisburg and Pemberton squares, both of which were created around the time that Bulfinch's square was becoming less sought after. Each of these squares was also enhanced by a small garden as its centerpiece.

Although Bulfinch's Franklin Place was a bold and unusual experiment in urban planning in this country, it was not unique. Another noteworthy garden square (conceived only ten years after Franklin Place) appeared in New York City in 1803 when Trinity Church planned St. John's Park—later called Hudson Square—in lower Manhattan. Expecting that a handsome structure would increase not only the value of its land but also the desirability of this Hudson River location to prospective residents, Trinity Church first erected St. John's Chapel on the property in 1804. Designed by John McComb, who is considered one of New York's most important Federal architects, the chapel was erected on the Varick Street side of the square. As noted earlier, the presence of a church either within or

Franklin Street looking west, ca. 1860s.

Carte-de-visite published by Joseph Ward & Son, Boston. Courtesy of The Bostonian Society/Old State House.

In this view, only one elm is left as a reminder of the garden that had once graced Franklin Place. The buildings shown on both sides of Franklin Street—as well as the lonely elm—were destroyed during the Great Fire of 1872, which spread throughout much of the downtown area.

very near a garden square was considered an amenity for the residents. London's St. James's Square had St. James's, Piccadilly, designed by Christopher Wren, one block away; and Bulfinch designed Holy Cross Church (1800) at one end of Franklin Place. With its locked garden of several acres and its surrounding red-brick row houses, by 1828 St. John's Park was much more similar in appearance to its London prototypes than was Franklin Place with its tiny garden and elegant Bulfinch-designed buildings. But St. John's Park was just as short-lived.

Hoping to retain the same kind of control as that held by London estate owners, the Trinity vestry first offered the lots with ninety-nine-year leases accompanied by building restrictions. Unfortunately the wealthy New Yorkers whom the vestry wished to attract were not interested in this remote location in the city, which was much farther north than the then-fashionable Bowling Green area at the lower tip of Manhattan. They also might not have liked the fact that the square was clearly modeled on a British prototype. As a result, the church, unlike many London estate owners, was not successful in leasing the lots to speculative builders. The project lay dormant, with St. John's Chapel standing alone in marshland until 1827, when the church decided to offer the sixty-four house lots for sale (instead of trying to lease them) and to deed the central space intended for a

Franklin Street, 2001.

Franklin Street at the former site of Franklin Place now has two oddly shaped traffic islands for pedestrians who cannot cross a wide street within the time allowed by the traffic lights. The two buildings (the one in the foreground was built in 1873, and the other in 1912) bordering Arch Street on the right are now occupied by banks.

garden to the property owners. More than twenty years after the square was originally planned there finally was much interest in it, and the church's effort was successful. Unlike Bulfinch, who went bankrupt from building his houses before they were all sold, the church was in a better financial position to wait for the appropriate market to develop.

By late 1828, the new property owners had enclosed their private garden with a tall iron fence costing $25,000 and had planted more than two hundred varieties of trees, ornamental shrubs, and flowers. In 1832, Frances Trollope, in her popular book *Domestic Manners of the Americans*, noted that St. John's Park was "beautiful, excellently well planted with a great variety of trees, and only wanting our frequent and careful mowing to make it equal to any square in London." She was impressed by the height of the iron fence as well as by the fact that the gravel for the walks had come from Boston as freight rather than ballast. In her view, however, the extreme uniformity of the red-brick Federal row houses detracted from the square's appearance.

During the 1830s and early 1840s, St. John's Park was the city's most fashionable address, although the relatively small and architecturally restrained row houses did not lend themselves to the kind of elegant entertaining to which Mrs. Trollope was accustomed. She had noted that the dining and drawing rooms of the houses were on the same floor, a layout that prevented more refined and sophisticated mixed dinner parties of ladies and gentlemen. The more usual arrangement was an upstairs drawing room to which the women could *withdraw* (hence the earlier term *withdrawing room*) to make tea while the men remained in the dining room to drink and talk politics before joining the women. Mrs. Trollope would certainly have approved of the placement of the parlors on the second floor and the dining room on the first floor of the house in Franklin Place that Sargent had painted.

By the mid-1840s, the neighborhood began to deteriorate as a result of encroaching warehouses and railroad tracks. Finally, in 1866, Cornelius Vanderbilt purchased the garden, paying Trinity Church $400,000 and each property owner $13,000 for his share of the garden. A year later, after having all of the two hundred trees removed, Vanderbilt erected on the sight a freight depot for the Hudson River Railroad. The once-fashionable row houses that had formerly overlooked a beautiful garden soon became rooming houses facing a freight depot. The residents of St. John's Park had sold their impressive garden to a commercial venture, even though the square was not located close to a burgeoning business district. In many respects the demise of St. John's Park resembled the loss of

Boston's Franklin Place eight years earlier. The property owners in Boston's Franklin Place had readily sold their Bulfinch houses to the city, which immediately turned the property over to commercial developers.

Louisburg Square

Toward the end of the eighteenth century, as business prospered, the population of Boston began to expand dramatically, with the result that there was now a perceived need for another residential area to accommodate newly successful merchants. In 1795, when the Bulfinch-designed State House on Beacon Hill was under construction, a syndicate of wealthy individuals calling themselves the Mount Vernon Proprietors began buying up land on Mount Vernon, the peak to the west of Beacon Hill. Of these twenty acres—owned by the expatriate painter John Singleton Copley and sold through his agent, Gardiner Greene—most were hilly upland pasture that had little value before construction of the State House. In order to develop Copley's former estate the Proprietors would have to undertake a massive grading operation. The summit of Beacon Hill had already been cut down for the State House, and Pemberton Hill to the east would soon be reduced to create Pemberton Square.

Bulfinch, initially a member of this syndicate, resigned in 1797 because of financial difficulties associated with Franklin Place. However, in 1796 he had drawn up a plan for the entire property, showing large lots intended for freestanding houses with stables and gardens. This plan, which was never adopted, provided for a large open square measuring 460 feet by about 190 feet, with three streets running into it. This plan testified to Bulfinch's interest in landscapes as important components of residential development and probably influenced the plan for Louisburg Square that eventually was adopted.

After twenty-five years, during which the Mount Vernon Proprietors sold the bulk of their property to affluent buyers who would erect large mansions, the syndicate members were ready to develop the final piece of their property, which came to be called Louisburg Square.

Bulfinch's earlier plan for a garden square may have seemed like the ideal blueprint for a profitable real estate venture. The Proprietors probably were aware of London's beautiful garden squares, and Bulfinch's elegant Franklin Place also must have impressed them. The major difference between the two developments would be economic: Franklin Place was conceived as a tontine association in which participants bought shares, whereas the Proprietors' lots were to be sold outright before houses were built. Franklin Place had caused Bulfinch to go bankrupt because he and his partners had financed construction of the houses well before subscribers bought shares in the venture. Both of these projects differed from the previously described traditional leasehold system used in developing the London estates, according to which the buyers purchased buildings from speculative builders but signed leases with the landowner.

In 1826, the Proprietors adopted a plan, drawn up by surveyor S. P. Fuller, for developing the western end of the block formed by Pinckney, Sumner (now Mount Vernon), Joy, and West Cedar streets. The entire property sloped down from east to west. The plan called for narrow lots that were intended only for attached dwellings. These would generate more income for the Proprietors than larger lots would. Since private stables were to be grouped elsewhere in the neighborhood, the lots did not back onto service alleys, as the lots in Franklin Place did. In the interest of economizing on space, the Proprietors must have believed that private alleys with stables would not be important to prospective buyers.

The name given to the square is thought to have commemorated Sir William Pepperrell's capture of the French fortress of Louisburg in Nova Scotia in 1745, a battle that ensured England's dominance on the Atlantic seaboard. Unlike St. John's Park in New York, where there initially was some reluctance among prospective residents to replicate an English style of living, Bostonians did not seem to mind making this connection. Because of its small size and location on the last part of Mount Vernon to be developed, Louisburg Square became a buffer offering protection from the less-desirable residential development on the north side of the hill. The square also served as a fitting symbol of the transition from a neighborhood of freestanding houses to one that included fashionable row houses.

It is interesting to note the contrast between the lifestyle of Harrison Gray Otis (1765–1848), one of the Mount Vernon Proprietors and a successful lawyer, and that envisioned by the Proprietors for the first residents of Louisburg Square. On the one hand, by the time Otis was thirty he was able to commission Bulfinch to design a freestanding mansion for him. This proved to be the first of three freestanding mansions that Bulfinch would create for him as the years passed. (The first, now the headquarters of the Society for the Preservation of New England Antiquities, is located in what was formerly called the West End at the foot of Beacon Hill. The second, built in 1802, is situated on the ridge of Mount Vernon, now 85 Mount Vernon Street. The third, built in 1806 at 45 Beacon Street, overlooks the Common and, like its predecessors, has a separate side entrance opening onto a carriageway and carriage house. In addition to these in-town mansions, Otis also had a country estate in Watertown, where he spent his summers entertaining. By contrast, the only amenity that the plan for Louisburg Square offered to prospective residents was a common garden space with long, straight sides and short, bowed ends, a space that was wider but not much larger than Franklin Place's elongated semi-oval garden.

The deed dividing the land among the original four Proprietors stipulated that the area designated for a garden should be forever kept open but could be surrounded by a fence or railing. The two streets (each forty feet wide) that ran alongside the garden were intended to be conveyed to the city at a later date. This plan indicated that initially the Proprietors' model was Franklin Place with its public streets rather than London squares with their private streets. The new residents later had a change of heart regarding the streets of Louisburg Square.

The initial phase of the project moved slowly, suggesting that the narrow lots intended for attached dwellings may have been over-priced and, therefore, unattractive to builders who would need to find affluent buyers for their houses. This same reluctance to live in row houses had made the detached double houses of Bulfinch's Franklin Place more popular than the attached dwellings of his crescent, despite the higher selling prices of the detached houses. In Franklin Place all twenty-four houses were erected and sold by Bulfinch and his partners in five years, but in Louisburg Square the process of first selling the lots and then building the houses took much longer. The first lot of Louisburg Square was not sold and built upon until 1834, almost ten years after the plan was drawn up. However, by the summer of 1844, houses had been erected on most of the twenty-eight lots, including the seven on Pinckney Street at the northern end of the square. Properties on the Mount Vernon Street side of the square were not considered part of the square because several row houses were already there when the Proprietors' plan was adopted.

By the time most of the houses in Louisburg Square were built between 1834 and 1844, the architectural styles represented on Mount Vernon had changed dramatically from Bulfinch's days. After his work on Franklin Place, Bulfinch went on to design several freestanding mansions as well as some small groups of row houses on Beacon Hill before he left for Washington in 1817 to serve as Architect of the Capitol under President Monroe. His departure left no one of stature to carry on the neoclassical tradition he had brought to Boston. Asher Benjamin was a Bulfinch disciple and author of the popular *American Builder's Companion* (1806), a source book on the Federal style, and the *Practice of Architecture* (1833). Benjamin championed the Greek Revival style, which was well represented in the row houses of Louisburg

Square. This style was characterized by simplicity of forms and ornament, including rectangular lintels over windows and pediment-shaped lintels over front doors.

The decade from 1819 to 1829 had seen the increased construction of row houses in the Beacon Hill area, most of them the work of builder-architects who relied on pattern books. The resulting houses were relatively simple and uniform, with few wooden external decorative details. Between 1830 and 1840, bowed fronts, which until this time had been used only on Beacon Street near the State House, became common. The windows in these gently curved bays permitted more light to enter a room and promoted a sense of closer connection to the outside. The use of bowed or "swelled" fronts distinguished Boston's row houses from their counterparts in New York, Philadelphia, and Baltimore.

In most cases residents of Louisburg Square purchased their houses directly from contractors, who had purchased lots from the original Proprietors or their heirs and then erected houses on speculation. However, in 1847 the wealthy merchant Thomas Handasyd Perkins, Jr., who lived in a freestanding house at 1 Joy Street on Beacon Hill and also owned a country house in Brookline, built 2 Louisburg Square, one of the last houses to be constructed there, and immediately sold it to James P. Higginson. Since many different contractors constructed the houses in Louisburg Square over a period of ten years, the overall appearance of the houses on either side of the garden was not as uniform as that of later Boston row houses, where one contractor often bought many adjoining lots. The original deed stipulated only that all dwelling houses should be constructed of brick or stone. Although the deed did not contain any height restrictions, in the interest of uniformity the various builders maintained the same building height for each side.

In adopting Fuller's plan for Louisburg Square, the Mount Vernon Proprietors did not attempt to make the square level, with the result that even the garden sloped from east to west. The dwellings on the lower side of the square were primarily three-story bowfronts with an additional areaway that allowed light to enter the basement under the front stairs. Here the tallest windows were on the first floor just above the basement. Several of these houses had pediment-shaped lintels above their front doors; others had simple, rectangular lintels. On the upper side of the square most, but not all, of the four-story dwellings had flat fronts, many with cast-iron balconies running across the taller second-floor windows. This use of cast iron broke up the monotony of the brick façades and supplied much-needed decorative detail and three-dimensional interest. All the houses in the square had granite steps as well as granite basement levels.

An 1844 agreement among the new residents in the square, who also referred to themselves as "proprietors," acknowledged that the owners of the adjoining lots had the benefit of the private garden and that it would be appropriate for them to "enlarge and adorn" the "mall." The agreement also stipulated that there be a committee responsible for assessing each owner an equal share of all expenses related to "altering, enlarging and embellishing" the space and for overseeing the care of the small private garden. This arrangement, similar to the covenants in English leases that obligated lessees to pay for the upkeep of the gardens, was intended to run with the land and extend to subsequent proprietors. Although Louisburg Square's garden was relatively small compared to its London counterparts, it rapidly assumed a role in the proprietors' lives that was disproportionate to its size. Because the new proprietors kept minutes of all their meetings after they signed the 1844 agreement, it is possible to trace the history of the garden from that time until the present.

The garden in Louisburg Square was immediately enlarged 10 feet in length and 8 feet in width, reaching its present dimensions of approximately 225 feet by 48 feet, with an area of 10,800 square feet. This improvement reflected the proprietors' perception of the garden as an important amenity. Within a year they installed a new cast-iron fence—the defining symbol of exclusivity common to all London squares—along with four lampposts. The design for the fence, which appeared in the proprietors' *Records* as a freehand drawing rather than a pattern from a catalog, included five-foot Egyptian Revival lotus-stalk posts mounted on one-foot-high granite bases. The committee in charge of commissioning the fence decided to dispense with a gateway or opening in the fence, thereby discouraging access to the garden. At the time, the issue of easy access for maintenance was not considered important enough to warrant the inclusion of a gate. This decision was to cause extra work and expense in 1849, when a portion of the fence had to be removed in order to place two statues in the garden.

The early residents, who were attracted to Louisburg Square either by its convenience to downtown or its location within a fashionable neighborhood of mansions, were always frugal regarding expenses for the garden. In fact, they expected support from the public sector and had petitioned the mayor, without success, to help defray their expenses for the new fence. The expectation of public support created tension in 1851, when the garden was being embellished with a fountain. In 1850, shortly after the Cochituate Water Works had begun supplying water to Boston, the proprietors voted to begin constructing a fountain. Cast-iron fountains were popular during this period, and the proprietors saw no reason not to take advantage of this new water source, especially if the city would agree to pay for the water. In fact, the city was already planning several fountains as central features for the South End's garden squares.

In the spring of 1851 the proprietors, disturbed that the municipal water commissioners had questioned the city's willingness to supply free water for a privately owned fountain, communicated their concerns, indicating that they had incurred a very heavy expenditure for the square's embellishments, which, in turn, had substantially increased the city's assessment of each house. They also said that they had talked with the mayor before constructing the fountain and had been assured they would receive water whenever there was a surplus. Finally, they noted that the mayor had said that with its new fountain, Louisburg Square greatly enhanced the city and demonstrated the good taste and public spirit of Boston's citizens.

In August 1851 the board of water commissioners notified the proprietors that it had no authority to allow private fountains to run without their owners making payment according to the water rates established by the city council. In December the city engineer conveyed to the mayor his cost estimate for running the fountain, and the mayor immediately sent a copy to the proprietors, with a personal note suggesting that they could adjust the time the fountain would run so that the expense would not be too burdensome.

The fountain appears to have run for only two seasons, the fall of 1850 and the summer of 1851. The only visual record of the fountain is an engraving of Louisburg Square that appeared in a local newspaper in 1851, depicting a three-tiered cast-iron fountain in a large, circular basin. In January 1852, the proprietors voted to confer again with the city about supplying water to the fountain at no charge. Considering the tone of the dispute, it is not surprising that in 1856, the proprietors voted to fill the basin with earth and plant flowers there. By that time the actual fountain must have already been removed.

There were other instances of tension between the proprietors of Louisburg Square and the public sector, particularly regarding the use of the two streets running along the garden's length. Although the original plan stipulated that the streets ultimately were to be given to the city, the proprietors did not take long in deciding that they preferred to keep these streets private. In 1855 and 1875 they put up temporary fences across these two streets of the square to indicate their intentions. In 1895 they recorded a public notice stating that the streets were to be forever private. On several later occasions the proprietors posted "Private Way" signs. However, they never gated their streets, as was commonly done in London's garden squares.

The implications of their decision to keep the streets private were perhaps greater than the proprietors had anticipated. Over the years

the proprietors had to fund repairs to the gutters, the two roadways, and the sidewalks around the square. They also had to deal with parking-related issues, such as restricting the number of proprietors' cars that were allowed in the square. The parking problem might never have become so serious if Louisburg Square had been provided with service alleys, as other squares in both London and Boston had been.

Louisburg Square, although inspired in part by the only local example of a garden square—Franklin Place—had more in common with late-seventeenth- and early-eighteenth-century English garden squares, particularly in the plain appearance of its dwellings and the simple design of its garden space. The image of Louisburg Square in the May 31, 1851, issue of *Gleason's Pictorial Drawing-Room Companion* shows the fountain and also depicts a double row of trees, grass, and the six-foot statues of Aristides and Columbus that had recently been placed at each end of the garden. The accompanying description could just as well have referred to a London square:

> The engraving represents a beautiful location in the western section of our city, surrounded by the residences of many of our most distinguished and fashionable families. This place affords one among many evidences that taste and refinement are gradually beautifying our city,

Louisburg Square, Boston. *Gleason's Pictorial Drawing-Room Companion.* May 31, 1851. Private collection.

The short-lived fountain in Louisburg Square, the statue of Columbus in the foreground facing Pinckney Street, and Aristides the Just at the opposite end of the garden are visible in this engraving. The fence has been simplified and does not show the beautiful Egyptian Revival lotus-stalk posts with the four attached lampposts.

Louisburg Square south to Mt. Vernon, ca. 1880s. Courtesy of The Bostonian Society/ Old State House.

This photo of Louisburg Square was taken looking from Pinckney Street to Willow Street, the only street entering the square from either the north or the south. Most of the eighteen original elm trees in the garden are visible, and none appear to be suffering from the various tree diseases that were soon to affect them.

and by-and-by Boston will present many outdoor specimens of the fine arts worthy of her character as the literary emporium and Athens of America.

Interestingly, the article refers to the original residents as "distinguished" and "fashionable"—precisely the types of residents that the developers of London squares had sought to attract. Bulfinch, too, had wanted to lure this type of resident, advertising "elegant" houses and a "convenient" location. But the original Proprietors, by offering small house lots without room for adjoining stables, in a location fairly remote from the downtown business area, had taken a chance that such wealthy buyers might not be attracted.

In 1844, clergymen, doctors, men of letters, and lawyers were counted among the proprietors in residence, along with several merchants, one of whom was George Richard Minot, whose Boston firm was a leading East India mercantile house. For most of the proprietors, who were affluent enough to own country estates as well, their town houses, just like those in most London squares, would not have been their full-time dwellings. The residents of Louisburg Square have often been solid and respectable families but were not always the most socially prominent ones in Boston. For more than a century three of the houses served as a convent for an order of Episcopal nuns. The square has been the scene of many colorful social events, such as the marriage of Jenny Lind, the famous singer, to her accompanist in 1852, and the "grandest party in Boston," hosted by Mayor Frederick

Lincoln in 1860. In 1932, Louisburg Square was the appropriate, although small, setting for the scene in the movie *Vanity Fair* in which the marriage of Becky Sharp took place in the garden of London's largest square, Russell Square.

Over the years the proprietors have sought to preserve the overall simplicity and regularity of the garden's original layout of trees and grass—hallmarks of English garden squares. Periodically concerns have been raised about the health of the elm trees and the grass. The proprietors have had to prune the trees and replace those that have become infected by various diseases. Although the garden originally contained eighteen elm trees planted in two rows, there currently are seventeen trees of different species: five elms, three lindens, four honey locusts, and five zelkovas. In such a small space this assortment of trees detracts from the overall integrity of the original design, yet planting a variety of trees ensures protection against diseases affecting one particular species. The proprietors had occasionally discussed adding flowers and shrubs; consequently seventeen types of shrubs, mostly flowering ones, were planted in 1935. In an effort to return to the original simplicity of the garden design, however, the proprietors

Louisburg Square, in a photograph by Bernice Abbott, ca. 1930.
Boston Athenæum.

When this photograph of Louisburg Square was taken, some of the original diseased American elms had been replaced with young English elms, which were thought to be more disease resistant. Also, the automobile had begun to be a permanent fixture in the square, making the residential enclave less attractive.

Louisburg Square, 1954, in a
photograph by Nishan
Bichajian.
Nishan Bichajian, Courtesy of
Kepes/Lynch Collection. Rotch
Visual Collections, M.I.T.

This photograph, also taken looking toward Pinckney Street, shows the
same beautiful elm tree in the foreground as the ca. 1930 photograph.
In addition to the many cars, most of them parked on the garden side of
the street because of the snow, this view shows the shrubbery planted
around the statue of Aristides in 1935.

have since removed most of these shrubs. The few remaining yews and rhododendrons are now quite overgrown and add a feeling of green lushness to the garden. In addition, they obscure views into the garden through the fence at the ends by passers-by on Mount Vernon and Pinckney streets.

The garden in Louisburg Square has historically functioned as an ornament to be viewed rather than accessed by the residents. Only in 1929 did the proprietors agree to install a small gate in the eastern side of the fence, and when keys were issued, their use was restricted. In 1946 two benches were placed in the garden, nestled within the shrubs at either end. Even if entry had been encouraged, it is not likely that many of the residents would have chosen to relax in such a small garden space, which—without shrubs in its early days— was quite open to public view. Yet the tall iron fence and the well-manicured grass, which is rarely crushed by footsteps, help to convey the atmosphere of privacy and exclusivity typical of London's squares. Nowadays, just as in Louisburg Square, views into the gardens of most London squares are often obscured by the shrubbery planted inside the fences, with the result that the occasional abutters who use the gardens for sitting, reading, or dog walking are protected from the eyes of passers-by.

Not only have the dwellings and the garden in Louisburg Square not changed dramatically in appearance over the course of 155 years, but the nature and interests of the proprietors as an ownership group have not changed significantly. The proprietors have continued to focus on preserving the integrity of the space, even though they have added shrubs, benches, and flowers. Periodically some proprietors have suggested putting another fountain in the garden, but as soon as the subject of paying for the water has come up, the idea has been rejected. A new fountain replicating the one that briefly graced the garden in the mid-nineteenth century might be appropriate but would require that the proprietors reach a consensus on both its design and the cost of operating it. On several occasions, having been over-whelmed by the expense of maintaining the fence, streets, and even the lawn, the proprietors have considered ceding some control to the city, but each time they have reaffirmed their commitment to owning and managing their entire property.

The *New York Times* has termed Louisburg Square "the most trea-sured trophy neighborhood in Boston" because it has attracted wealthy individuals who have sought the prestige of living in one of the twenty-eight town houses where the owners are also entitled to control of the streets and the garden. Since the design of each of the buildings was quite ordinary for its time, with the façades barely dis-tinguishable from one another, the attraction of Louisburg Square is

Louisburg Square, 2001.

As is evident in this photograph, Louisburg Square now includes a wide variety of trees, which create a dense canopy that casts shade on the grass. The overgrown shrubs around the statue of Columbus almost obscure one of the two benches placed in the garden in 1945.

probably not the individual dwellings. There are far more impressive buildings elsewhere in the vicinity and in the Back Bay. It also is unlikely that the tiny enclosed garden serves as the magnet drawing affluent families to the neighborhood. More likely it is the combination of all the signature components of a traditional garden square—the garden, the surrounding uniform architecture, the private streets, and the ambiance of exclusivity—that makes Louisburg Square the "trophy neighborhood" it has become.

Louisburg Square is a Boston icon for two reasons. It is a vestige from the past, having changed very little in its 155-year history, and a contemporary example of a small, wealthy group of individuals choosing to live in close quarters overlooking a common garden space in a residential district within walking distance of the downtown business area. In 1920, Hobart Winkley, longtime clerk of the proprietors, described the timeless attraction of the square in his unpublished *Annals*: "It is sincerely to be desired that Louisburg Square shall long retain its character of quaint simplicity with its air of private, quiet restfulness which it has so long enjoyed amid the inroads of modernity."

Over the years, whenever the economy was in a downturn, the professions and financial status of the individuals occupying the houses changed, with the single-family houses being altered for multi-family use. However, during the prosperous late 1990s the square came full circle, with many of its affluent residents occupying single-family houses. Because Louisburg Square is located in a residential neighborhood on the side of Beacon Hill farthest from the business district, its proprietors have not had to contend with the possibility of commercial encroachment, which ultimately became an unfortunate reality for the residents of Franklin Place and Pemberton Square.

London's St. James's Square

Whether or not the inspiration for Louisburg Square, like that of Franklin Place, can be traced to London squares is not as important as the fact that its distinguishing features as a garden square and its history over the years have much in common with London's earliest squares. The *Records* of Louisburg Square's proprietors have made it possible to compare the proprietors' concerns and activities regarding the upkeep of their garden over a 155-year period to the concerns and activities of the St. James's Square's trustees, who began keeping records in 1726. Ever since Lord St. Albans sold rather than leased his house lots in St. James's Square, the maintenance and management of the garden have been the responsibility of the trustees, or owners of the houses, rather than the owner of the entire estate. Even though the garden in Louisburg Square is one-tenth the size of the two-and-a-half-acre St. James's Square garden, the landscape issues confronting both groups of owners have always been similar in scope.

As mentioned earlier, in 1844, the Louisburg Square proprietors agreed that each would pay his share of the costs for enlarging and embellishing the garden as well as his share of all future expenses for repairs and enhancements. Through a 1726 Act of Parliament, St. James's Square's trustees were given permission by the Crown to assess themselves at a "rate sufficient to clean, adorn, and beautify the said square, and to continue the same in repair." This famous St. James's Square Act was the first to regulate a London square, and it is the only such act that remains unchanged to the present day. Despite annual assessments, the history of each garden has been marked by much discussion about the cost of improvements and repairs. Implicit in these discussions has always been the temptation, to which a few owners have always yielded, to suggest ceding some responsibilities to the public sector in order to lessen the financial burden of caring for their garden.

The Louisburg Square proprietors never gave their streets to the city, as they had originally intended. In contrast, by 1860 the trustees of St. James's Square had handed over to other agencies, both public and private, all responsibilities relating to the carriageway and footpaths. The most significant result of this loss of authority over matters outside the fence was that the residents' assessments were slashed, with the consequence that less money was available for maintaining and improving the garden. By 1911, with the garden totally overgrown, the trustees agreed to allow the Commission of Works to take over ownership of the statue of King William III (1689–1702), which had been installed in 1808.

World War II had a delayed effect on St. James's Square. After having sold their iron perimeter fence for scrap metal during the war, in 1972 the trustees became anxious to replace the chain-link fence that had been installed subsequently with a new iron one. However, having found it difficult to raise the private funds necessary for this project, they were faced with the prospect of handing over their garden to the Westminster City Council. After much discussion, which was complicated by the issue of who actually owned the garden, the majority reached an agreement that the garden would receive better protection from the trustees than it would from public agencies. In March 1974, a resolution was carried by a vote of 8 to 7 that the trustees should continue managing the garden. In return for receiving public funds to finance the construction of a new fence, the trustees offered to open the garden to the public on weekdays. The garden already had been open to the public at lunchtime since the 1930s, when a royal commission encouraged making London's squares more accessible to the public.

Just as the proprietors of Louisburg Square had problems with a fountain, the trustees of St. James's Square had a basin 150 feet in diameter that was to plague them from 1727 until its removal in 1854. Surrounded by an octagonal iron fence, the fountain consisted of a single *jet d'eau*, which emerged from a low, square plinth. When the fountain ceased to operate, the plinth was removed; and in 1808 the statue of King William III was placed on a pedestal in the center of the enormous basin. As late as 1849, a carpenter named Fitch was paid for constructing a punt to be used in cleaning the basin. With the exception of the lady in the gondola pictured in Nichols's ca. 1725 view of the square (see p. 4), this was the only recorded instance of boating in the basin. The filling of the basin with dirt in 1854 may have been the result of the trustees' ongoing frustration with the cost of keeping the water clean.

In Louisburg Square, except for some minor changes to the garden—the removal of the fountain, the replacement of elms with other tree species, and the addition of some shrubs and flowers—the overall appearance has remained almost unchanged for 155 years.

St. James's Square, on the other hand, has undergone some very dramatic landscape changes throughout its long history. The first significant planting of grass did not occur until 1759 when it was used to replace the gravel surrounding the basin inside the railing. In 1817 the trustees asked the architect John Nash to submit a plan for the garden. Of the three alternative designs he proposed, the trustees preferred the one that retained the basin and added a ten-foot-wide belt of shrubs within an enlarged perimeter fence. Nash's design did not include trees, but in 1825 the trustees voted to introduce "a few forest trees." For many years after the basin was filled in 1854, nothing more was done to improve the appearance of the garden.

In 1911, upon assuming ownership of the statue of William III, the Commission of Works made several recommendations for improving the garden. These included more flower beds and a new planting design, which would permit the statue to be viewed from the surrounding roads. Plans were soon made to reconfigure the curved paths into four straight approaches to the statue, but these plans were not implemented until 1922, when one of the residents paid for the recommended landscape improvements. By 1985 a new landscape plan had been created by popular landscape designer John Brookes and then implemented. This design featured the addition of many varieties of flowering shrubs as well as a circle of rose bushes around the statue.

In the late 1990s the garden was totally redesigned to reflect the layout as it had been in 1854 after the removal of the basin. The statue now sits in the middle of a circular grass plat—probably of the same diameter as the old basin—surrounded by a circular path. All the rose bushes and flowering shrubs have been removed. In other words, the garden has essentially been returned to its nineteenth-century design, which featured all the traditional elements in a London garden square (a black iron perimeter fence, curved paths, trees, and grass) and with the original nineteenth-century statue of King William III at its center.

The issue of access is one that both groups of owners have had to deal with, although one garden is large and the other quite small. In Louisburg Square the installation of the first of two gates in 1929 was accompanied by strict regulations: each proprietor was allowed only one key, children under the age of ten were not allowed in the garden without an adult, and games that might ruin the grass were prohibited. In 1946 the proprietors installed two benches in the garden, thereby indicating that they did not object to having the space used by parents and small children. For about ten years after the benches were installed the proprietors discussed providing a sandbox, but this suggestion was finally rejected.

Before the St. James's Square garden was opened to the public at lunch hour in the 1930s, there had been several periods when the trustees allowed bicycles, perambulators, dogs, and even lawn-tennis players. Since then the trustees have managed to keep the garden relatively free of activities that could damage the trees and grass. In recent years they have permitted the garden to be used for occasional receptions, plays, or concerts. In 1975, when there was talk of using the garden for a sculpture exhibition that might attract up to 175,000 people, the sculptor Henry Moore managed to derail the plan by saying that the trees, which were "sculptures in themselves," would compete with the man-made sculptures.

Just as Louisburg Square's proprietors have had to contend with parking issues, even though they own their streets, the St. James's Square trustees have been confronted with similar issues, both below and above ground. The trustees warded off the threat of underground parking garages in 1935, 1953, and 1962. Not as easy to control—in part because the trustees do not own the streets in the square—has been the increase in parking around the garden. Although the trustees have expressed their concern about damage to the trees and shrubs caused by gasoline fumes and have urged that drivers park with their tailpipes facing the buildings rather than the garden, they have not succeeded in having the parking regulations changed.

This comparison of the activities and concerns of the owners of the houses and gardens of two old squares—one in London and one in Boston—illustrates the similarity in the responsibilities associated with overseeing these historic landscapes. In both cases there has always been some tension between the private and public sectors regarding maintenance responsibilities. On several occasions the owners of both gardens—always motivated to save money—have tried to negotiate for additional services from the public sector.

The Louisburg Square proprietors and the St. James's Square trustees have for the most part always relied on volunteers to oversee ongoing maintenance tasks. Such tasks have been funded almost entirely by assessments levied on the owners of the abutting properties, and the owners historically have spent a good deal of time discussing what tasks they should fund and how much should be spent. The owners in both squares are very conscious of their heritage and have consistently made every effort to protect the integrity of their gardens. Since each garden has successfully weathered several controversial issues, it is likely that both gardens will be preserved for a long time to come.

Other than Boston's Louisburg Square, the only prominent square in the United States that is still a private garden square in the London tradition is New York's Gramercy Park. Both squares were created almost contemporaneously as second-generation squares within their respective cities. Gramercy Park, laid out by Samuel Ruggles in 1831, may have been inspired by the success of St. John's Park, with its large garden, for Ruggles had not visited England. The garden in Gramercy Park is much larger than the one in Louisburg Square, and in appearance it is much more like the gardens found in London squares. Because the streets around Gramercy Park's garden have never been private, the owners have had to deal with many of the same traffic and parking issues that their St. James's Square counterparts have faced over the years.

Located between 19th Street and 22nd Street—farther uptown than St. John's Park—Gramercy Park was designed as a two-acre garden surrounded by sixty house lots. Ruggles stipulated that five trustees would oversee the park for life. By the late 1830s the trustees had erected a fence around the garden, which required a key for access, and had planted it with privet hedges and fifty kinds of trees and shrubs. By 1848 they had installed a simple fountain. Just as London's private squares tended to attract affluent and notable residents, Gramercy Park soon became home to a host of prominent people. Among its famous residents were Cyrus Field, who laid the transAtlantic cable; Samuel Tilden, presidential candidate and one of the founders of the New York Public Library; Stanford White, architect; Peter Cooper, philanthropist; and Edwin Booth, the well-known actor. A statue of Booth was installed in the center of the garden in 1918, replacing the 1848 fountain, which was then moved to another location on the same property.

In recent years conflicts among the trustees of Gramercy Park have centered on access to the garden and on some significant landscape issues. The garden is open to the public only during the May plant sale, but several trustees have advocated allowing access for musical events and art exhibits, and even for movie shoots that might provide needed revenue for the garden. The most contentious issue, however, was whether or not to prune or remove many of the old trees, whose dead branches had occasionally fallen to the ground. Lawsuits were filed for and against pruning and removal. In 1995 a major redesign of the park was proposed, at an estimated cost of $755,000. The landscape plan covered new trees, hedges, and flowers as well as post-and-chain fences and the repair and repainting of the perimeter fence. Although opponents of this design—a group constituting at least half of the abutters—feared that the garden would be transformed from the existing naturalistic English style to a more formal Italianate style, the new design was eventually implemented.

As in Louisburg Square, the houses facing the garden in Gramercy

Park have become very desirable. Although there are now almost five hundred housing units in the square, the turnover of residents has been low. Property overlooking the garden has always been priced higher than the nearby houses, which are often considered part of the "Gramercy Park neighborhood" because of the prestige associated with the square. In 1995 the president of the Gramercy Park Block Association, which monitors safety and quality-of-life issues, noted, "The neighborhood is an urban oasis. It's what urban living should be. There are tons of high-powered people living here, but they come to escape the glamour and the confusion."

Pemberton Square

Pemberton Square, the third of Boston's downtown squares, is the least known of the three, not just because it lasted only fifty years but also because neither its buildings nor its garden were in any way significant. Franklin Place, which did not last much longer than Pemberton Square, could boast houses designed by Charles Bulfinch. Louisburg Square, which outlived the other squares by more than a hundred years because it was never in the path of commercial development, has a relatively large garden compared to those of Franklin Place and Pemberton Square. However, despite the physical differences among these squares, their stories have several themes in common.

The socioeconomic forces that gave rise to the creation of Pemberton Square—its dwellings and the garden—were in most respects identical to the forces influencing the development of Franklin Place and Louisburg Square. All three garden squares were real estate ventures intended to generate a profit for their developers. A small garden in the center and a location near the business district were to be the special features that would attract prominent residents. The two squares that were so close to Boston's business center that they had little chance of remaining residential ultimately suffered an identical fate. Pemberton Square, like Franklin Place before it, could not remain a viable residential enclave. Houses on the west side of Pemberton Square were razed in 1885 to make way for the Suffolk County Courthouse, and those remaining on the east side suffered a similar fate in 1969 to make room for a large office building.

Between 1810 and 1850, Boston's population more than quadrupled, rising from 34,000 in 1810 to 137,000 in 1850. A burgeoning economy and a steady increase in immigrants from Europe accounted for this rapid growth. Just as the Mount Vernon Proprietors sought to take advantage of the need for more housing by using the peak to the west of Beacon Hill, a similar effort was made on Pemberton Hill, the eastern peak of the Trimountain. In the eighteenth century Pemberton Hill had attracted many prominent Boston residents, who built handsome mansions with gardens. Most impressive was the estate purchased in 1803 by Gardiner Greene, a wealthy banker who had married a daughter of John Singleton Copley. As has been mentioned earlier, Greene had been Copley's agent in the sale of the painter's property to the Mount Vernon Proprietors. Since the estate was on a slope, Greene had developed terraced gardens with ornamental trees, peacocks, and greenhouses.

After Greene's death in 1832, Patrick Tracy Jackson, one of the founders of the textile mills in Lowell and treasurer of the Boston and Lowell Railroad, purchased the property. Jackson intended to cut down the top of Pemberton Hill in order to create a desirable residential area halfway down the slope, at the point where the mansion had stood. This massive grading operation took only five months and was completed in October of 1835. Instead of simply hiring a surveyor, as the Mount Vernon Proprietors had done ten years earlier, Jackson sponsored a design competition for developing his property, which was bounded by Somerset Street to the west and Tremont Street to the east. Given the perceived financial success of nearby Franklin Place and Louisburg Square, Jackson may have suggested that his property include a garden square as an amenity. Alexander Wadsworth, a local civil engineer and surveyor and one of forty-seven entrants, won the $500 prize.

On October 6, 1835, Patrick Jackson put up for auction all of the sixty-five lots that Alexander Wadsworth had laid out—those on Tremont and Somerset streets as well as those fronting on a garden in Phillips Place, which was renamed Pemberton Square in 1838. As drawn on the plan, the house lots on both sides of Pemberton Square backed onto a second row of lots fronting on Tremont and Somerset streets, with only a six-foot passageway between the two rows. This meant that, just as in Louisburg Square, the house lots were not large enough to accommodate stables; in fact, stables were prohibited. In Jackson's new development not all of the lots were intended for residences. The auction catalog noted that the twenty-five lots facing on Tremont Street to the east would be good investments because they were conveniently situated for shops, public rooms, and offices. The lots suitable for dwelling houses were described as "not surpassed if equaled by any in the City for elevation, retirement, and proximity to business."

The garden square portion of Jackson's new development consisted of twenty-five lots, of which thirteen were in a crescent shape on the east side separated almost at the middle by the continuation of

Court Street, which entered the square. According to the plan most of the lots in Pemberton Square had frontages of between twenty-seven feet and twenty-nine feet. These frontages were similar in width to those of the row houses in Louisburg Square, Franklin Place, and even London's Bedford Square. It is interesting to compare the number of house lots included in each of Boston's downtown squares. Franklin Place had sixteen houses in the crescent and eight on the opposite side of the square. Louisburg Square had a total of twenty-one lots on the long sides and an additional seven lots at the Pinckney Street end. Pemberton Square's twenty-five lots fronted on a small, semi-oval garden that measured two hundred feet long and sixteen feet wide at its widest point. Two streets—thirty-four and thirty-nine feet wide, respectively (including nine-foot sidewalks in front of the houses)—bordered the garden.

The garden in Pemberton Square was only about half as wide as the garden in Franklin Place and eighty feet shorter, and it was a third as wide as and twenty-five feet shorter than Louisburg Square's garden. The auction prospectus stipulated that the purchasers of the lots fronting on the garden would have the responsibility of planting the garden and providing a suitable fence for it as well as for making repairs and keeping the garden in good condition. The owners of these lots were to be assessed equally for the expenses. The prospectus also suggested that each purchaser of a lot in Pemberton Square should fence in a small garden ten feet deep at the front edge of his lot and plant the area with grass or shrubs. Bulfinch's detached double buildings in Franklin Place also had small front gardens, but the row houses in Louisburg Square did not.

The garden, streets, and passageways as laid out on the plan were to remain forever open for the use and enjoyment of the residents. Because the dwellings fronting on the garden backed up to a second row of buildings fronting on either Tremont or Somerset Street, it is unlikely that nonresidents would have had a reason to use the smaller streets leading from these main streets to Pemberton Square. Nonetheless, the auction prospectus suggested that if three-quarters of the owners agreed, a gate could be erected at the end of the small street leading from Somerset Street. No record exists to show that a gate was ever installed. By permitting a gate, however, Jackson might have been revealing his familiarity with contemporary London squares, where the streets were gated.

The prospectus for Pemberton Square outlined in great detail how the square's infrastructure—streets, passageways, curbs, sidewalks, and drains—would be installed and maintained. Jackson was responsible for providing the infrastructure, with the owners of the abutting lots paying half his expenses. The fact that the cost of future maintenance was to be borne entirely by the abutters implied that Jackson considered the streets of Pemberton Square to be private, in contrast with the streets of Franklin Place. This arrangement differed only slightly from that set forth in the deed of the Mount Vernon Proprietors, which stipulated that all expenses related to installation of the sidewalks would be borne by the proprietors. The deed did not mention costs related to installing and maintaining Louisburg Square's two streets, which ultimately were to be ceded to the city.

Auctioning these lots was not much more successful than the sale of lots in Louisburg Square had been, a process that took many years. Deeds for the year 1835 show only about nine new owners for lots in Pemberton Square. Whether this was the result of the Panic of 1837 or the fact that the market for row houses in Boston had been saturated, records of deeds for the next few years do not show activity in Pemberton Square. Even though Jackson did not require that houses in Pemberton Square be erected immediately—allowing thirty years from the date of sale—his prospectus stipulated that "the style, elevation and plans of the fronts of all buildings, including fences," were to be determined by the majority of the owners within sixty days of the sale of the lots. If a new owner did not have a plan for his building, Jackson would agree to furnish one. On the straight side of the square, buildings of not fewer than three or more than four stories were required, whereas the curved side had no height restrictions. On either side of the square owners could choose to have "swelled or circular fronts," and these bays could extend three feet farther toward the line of the street.

The few early owners of lots must not have been inclined to build or to meet Jackson's deadline for submitting their plans. In 1836, Jackson commissioned George Minot Dexter (1802–1872) to design the houses for Pemberton Square and all the accompanying ironwork (stair railings, fences for the small front yards, and the fence with lampposts for the central garden). Dexter was a young architect whose only work experience was as an assistant engineer with the Boston and Lowell Railroad. By commissioning a set of uniform architectural plans, Jackson ensured that the buildings would be consistent in style and ornamentation as opposed to the less-uniform houses in Louisburg Square designed by several contractors.

Since the houses of both Pemberton and Louisburg squares were built during the same ten-year period and were similar in size—with almost the same number of row houses extending the length of the east and west sides of the gardens—it is instructive to compare their architectural styles. On the crescent-shaped east side of Pemberton Square the dwellings were three-story bowfronts with high basements and dormers. All these buildings had the same unadorned, rectangular

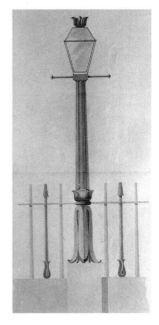

Design by George Dexter for a lamppost in Pemberton Square.

Dexter, vol. 3. Pemberton Square, p. 27, ca. 1836. Boston Athenæum.

This design by George Dexter, an architect, for the lamppost and fence in Pemberton Square is significant because it predates pattern books of cast-iron designs for such items. Compared to Louisburg Square's fence, Dexter's fence is shorter and, consequently, more appropriate for a smaller garden.

Pemberton Square,
ca. 1860, in a photograph
by Halliday.
Courtesy of the Society for the
Preservation of New England
Antiquities.

This photograph by Halliday
shows Dexter's lanterns, with
small embellishments, attached
to the fence around Pemberton
Square's garden. The garden is
clearly intended for viewing,
for there is not even a sidewalk
around it. The twenty-five-
year-old trees do not appear
healthy, and some young trees
can be seen within the garden.

lintels and plain pilasters, in contrast with several styles of pediment-shaped lintels and more prominent pilasters surrounding the entrances of many of the houses on Louisburg Square's west side. On the west side of Pemberton Square all the four-story flat fronts had iron balconies as an embellishment. These iron balconies appeared on the four-story flat fronts—and even some of the bowfronts—on the east side of Louisburg Square. Dexter's austere, utilitarian style—possibly the result of his engineering background and his lack of experience in designing houses—may have made these buildings less desirable than those in Louisburg Square. The only features breaking the monotony of the buildings on each side of Pemberton Square were the iron balconies on the flat fronts and the exuberant iron stair railings on the bowfronts.

Edwin Bacon, a prominent Boston journalist writing in 1883, just two years before most of Pemberton Square was demolished, describes the square's original attractions:

> In the middle of the square was an enclosed green, with a few trees, which was a pleasant bit of nature for the eye of the city man to rest upon. The dwellings built in it were fine, indeed elegant for their time, and for many years it was the residence of some of the most substantial citizens.

A photograph of Pemberton Square taken in 1885 reveals a garden

Old Pemberton Square,
ca. 1880, in a photograph
by Baldwin Coolidge.
Courtesy of the Society for the
Preservation of New England
Antiquities.

In this photograph, taken roughly twenty years later from the opposite
end of Pemberton Square, the lamppost is missing, but the trees appear
healthier. The Fine Tailoring and China & Glass Ware signs on two of
the buildings are evidence that commercial establishments have begun
to move into the square.

that had seen better days. Much of the fencing and three of the four original lampposts are gone, and only three elm trees seem to remain.

Although Pemberton Square may have attracted "some of the most substantial citizens," these citizens primarily were owners of small businesses, who may have appreciated the fact that they could live in such close proximity to their workplaces. In commissioning Dexter to design the buildings fronting on Tremont and Somerset streets as well as those for Pemberton Square, Jackson did not seem to intend a distinct difference in appearance between the locations, although his prospectus did note that Pemberton Square would contain a garden. As it turned out, since Dexter's buildings for Pemberton Square were not particularly distinguished and also backed onto buildings intended for businesses, buyers looking for an attractive neighborhood might have preferred the more prestigious residential location of Louisburg Square.

Bacon traces the gradual encroachment of businesses into Pemberton Square, writing that at first architects, lawyers, and other professionals established their offices there. They were followed by a

Pemberton Square,
ca. 1920.
Courtesy of the Boston Public Library, Print Department.

The Suffolk County Courthouse, built in 1891 on the west side of Pemberton Square, is shown on the left, while two large office buildings have been erected on the east side. The few original houses that were not demolished in 1885 have been taken over by businesses supporting the legal profession.

number of city and state offices, including the headquarters of the board of police commissioners. Photographs from this period depict trade signs on many of the buildings. As businesses moved in, the residents moved out, most often to the upscale Back Bay. Finally, in 1885, following several years of agitation by government officials in Boston for a new courthouse, the west side of Pemberton Square was razed to make room for the Suffolk County Courthouse. The garden was also eliminated at that time.

A few of the square's original dwellings on the east side survived until the autumn of 1969, when they, along with two more recent office buildings, were demolished and replaced by Center Plaza, a very long office building. The form of Center Plaza mirrored the entire crescent-shaped span of the original houses on the east side of the square, and the space between the courthouse and this monolithic structure was left open. This space is now a brick-and-concrete plaza dotted with trees in front of the courthouse and with some planters containing small trees and flowers. These landscape remnants serve as a perverse reminder of the ornamental garden that once graced the spot.

Although the garden in Pemberton Square was more truncated than the one in Franklin Place, the crescent-shaped open spaces of both squares, which included a street on either side of the garden,

Pemberton Square, 2001.

On the left is the new courthouse, built adjacent to the old courthouse and completed in 1939, and on the right, the Center Plaza office building. The space between the buildings is now paved with bricks, but there are not enough amenities to make the area an attractive destination for nearby workers.

were and still are very similar in size. The main difference between the spaces is that unlike the curved section of Franklin Street, which still has the potential to be a great urban space because of its unique shape and its connection to adjoining streets, today's Pemberton Square has been cut off completely from its surrounding streets. The street that originally entered the square from Somerset Street no longer exists, and the continuation of Court Street entering from the east is now a set of escalators carrying pedestrians up to the courthouse.

The most significant difference between Boston's three downtown garden squares and their London counterparts was size. The London estates were so large that their owners could afford to set aside ample spaces for garden squares. Even though a speculative real estate venture in the form of a garden square was new to them, they did not have much to lose in terms of either land or money. In Boston, on the other hand, space on the Shawmut Peninsula was at a premium, and those who wanted to enter into this kind of venture had more to lose. Charles Bulfinch, the first to transplant a garden square to Boston, had taken the greatest financial risk by constructing his buildings before they all were sold. As a result, he ended up bankrupt.

Although the financial impetus behind the creation of Boston's three downtown squares was the same, their differences mirrored the personalities and proclivities of their planners. The major differences among the squares, therefore, lay in the styles of their houses and gardens. The houses in Franklin Place were an architectural tour de force reflecting Bulfinch's interest and expertise in architecture. Although he appreciated the importance of gardens, he did not— and, in fact, could not—allow much space for one. Because the garden in Franklin Place was not intended to be private, the advertisements placed by Bulfinch and his partners for the property focused only on the proposed houses and their convenient location.

The developers of Louisburg and Pemberton squares, where the row houses were not architecturally distinguished, seemed more interested in focusing on the private garden as an amenity that would attract buyers. The garden in Louisburg Square, although small by London standards, was more substantial in size than those in the other two downtown squares. The Mount Vernon Proprietors were quite explicit about the future role of the owners in enhancing their garden. As it happened, this role grew larger over the years. In contrast, by hiring an inexperienced architect to design the houses in Pemberton Square and allotting only a tiny space for a garden, Patrick Jackson demonstrated that he was first and foremost an efficient businessman who was less concerned about aesthetic details. Yet Pemberton Square's auction prospectus did outline the responsibilities the new owners would have to assume in enhancing their garden as well as the method of assessments that would be used to pay for these improvements.

Although Franklin Place was an economic failure, it is easy to see that even though Bulfinch's primary motivation for engaging in this project may have been financial, in designing Boston's first garden square he focused most of his energy on creating a residential enclave that reflected his personal aspirations. By giving free space to both the Boston Library Society and the Massachusetts Historical Society and by building both the Boston Theatre and Holy Cross Church at one end of Franklin Place, Bulfinch was making a significant contribution to Boston's cultural life in the early Federal period. By the time the Mount Vernon Proprietors were ready to engage in their last real estate project on Mount Vernon, their focus was not so much on attracting Boston's elite as on making money. For the Proprietors, who had already sold most of their property to affluent buyers, many of whom soon erected large mansions, Louisburg Square was a mere afterthought. Ironically, its location in the middle of such a prestigious residential neighborhood was precisely the reason that Louisburg Square was the only one of Boston's three downtown squares to survive.

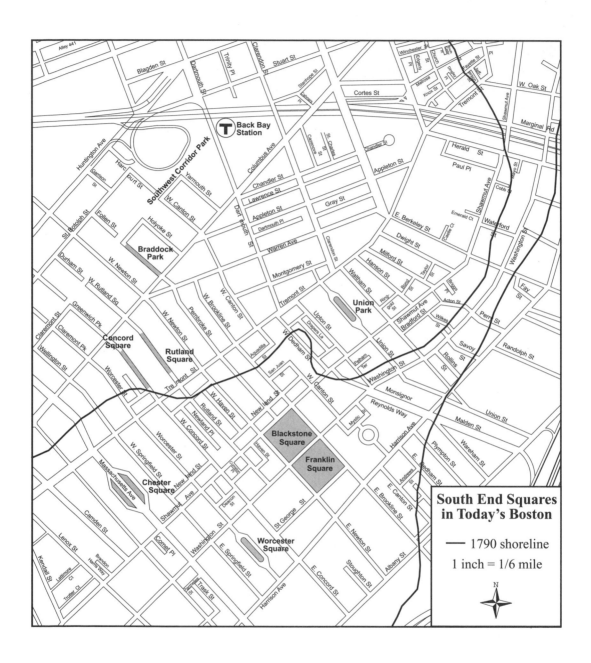

Alley 441

Blagden St

Trinity Pl

Clarendon St

Stuart St

Winchester St

Edgerly Pl

Church St

Fayette St

W. Oak St

Cortes St

Tremont St

Marginal Rd

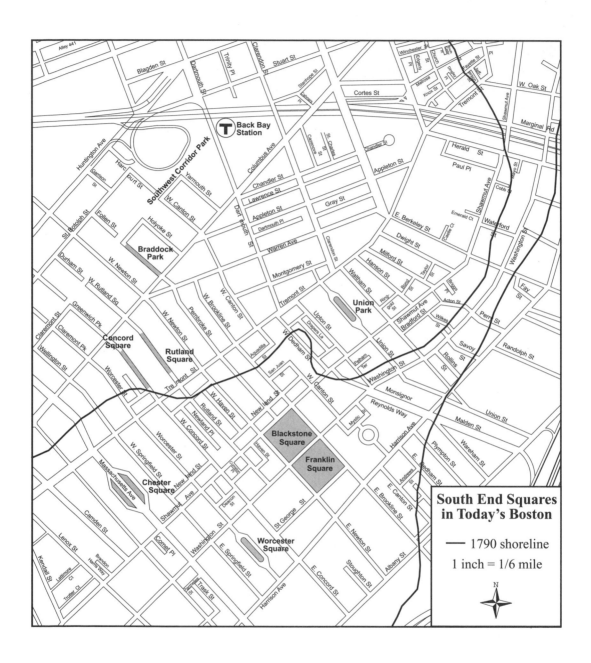

Back Bay Station

Huntington Ave

Harcourt St

Southwest Corridor Park

Yarmouth St

W. Canton St

Columbus Ave

St. Charles St

Cazenove St

Chandler St

Appleton St

Herald St

Paul Pl

Shawmut Ave

Chandler St

Lawrence St

Appleton St

Gray St

Garrison St

Folen St

Holyoke St

Dartmouth Pt

Warren Ave

E. Berkeley St

Emerald Ct

Castle Ct

Waterford St

Washington St

Cobb St

Botolph St

Braddock Park

Durham St

W. Newton St

Montgomery St

Tremont St

Dwight St

Clarendon St

Milford St

Hanson St

Waltham St

Taylor St

Bond St

Rodge St

Boggs St

Acton St

Fay St

Pern St

W. Rutland Sq

W. Brookline St

Pembroke St

W. Canton St

Union Park

Upton St

Shawmut Ave

Bradford St

Wilkes St

Greenwich Pk

Concord Square

W. Newton St

Aguadilla St

W. Dedham St

Draper La

Union St

Savoy St

Randolph St

Claremont St

Claremont Pk

Rutland Square

San Juan St

Batham Tier

Rollins St

Wellington St

Worcester St

Tremont St

W. Haven St

Newland St

Washington St

Monsignor

Union St

Malden St

Reynolds Way

Rutland St

W. Concord St

Blackstone Square

Mystic St

Harrison Ave

Plympton St

Wareham St

Massachusetts Ave

W. Springfield St

Worcester St

Newland Pl

Haven St

Franklin Square

E. Dedham St

Chester Square

New Hbd St

Andrews St

E. Canton St

E. Brookline St

Camden St

Shawmut Ave

Deacon St

St George St

E. Newton St

Albany St

Lenox St

Comet Pl

Washington St

E. Springfield St

Worcester Square

E. Concord St

Stoughton St

Kendall St

Lattimore Ct

Brandon Harris Way

Trask St

Harrison Ave

Trotter Ct

South End Squares in Today's Boston

—— 1790 shoreline

1 inch = 1/6 mile

N

Chapter Two

SOUTH END SQUARES

$\mathcal{I}$N ADDITION TO THE well-known Louisburg Square on Beacon Hill, Boston can boast a group of eight existing garden squares in its South End. This district, which now occupies about one square mile, was originally a narrow strip of land known as the "Neck," which connected Boston to Roxbury via Washington Street. Just as the Shawmut Peninsula was reshaped in the late eighteenth and early nineteenth centuries (when the Trimountain was cut down) to make way for new residential development, the Neck was enlarged with landfill—for the same purpose—beginning in the second quarter of the nineteenth century. The squares in the South End were created to help increase Boston's tax base by encouraging middle-class residents to remain in the city. At mid-century this group was attracted by the relatively spacious environs of the new garden suburbs, which were now accessible by improved modes of public transportation.

The significant difference between Boston's downtown squares and those in the South End was that all the South End squares were laid out by the city whereas each downtown square was created by a private developer. This difference had far-reaching implications that were to affect the gardens more than the houses in the squares. Because the city owned the gardens in the South End squares, it bore ultimate responsibility for their care. Over the years, however, there were occasions when the squares' residents were dissatisfied with the quality of the city's services and chose to supplement the municipal resources that were being dedicated to the gardens. In Louisburg Square the proprietors—the residents who owned the garden and were responsible for its care—sometimes expected the city to help, when, in fact, the city refused precisely because the garden and streets were privately owned.

For each developer of a downtown square, who obviously had thought that creating a garden square would be a profitable investment, this particular type of real estate venture was a one-time project—or even an experiment. In the South End, however, the city had more at stake. The city had the same financial goal as the private developers, yet the plan for achieving this goal entailed committing public funds in order to develop a significantly larger area with several strategically placed garden squares. The South End squares were unique in Boston because the city laid them out sequentially, thereby creating an entire group of garden squares.

Although the South End squares may have been inspired in part by London examples, only the first one—Columbia Square—can be traced to London through its creator, Charles Bulfinch, who was responsible for introducing London's garden-square form to downtown Boston. The city's motivation for creating a group of squares was similar to that of London's Bloomsbury Estate landowner, on whose property seven garden squares ultimately were built. Because of their relatively small size, garden squares could be laid out as needed without a great commitment of time or space. In both Bloomsbury and the South End the squares were usually located at least several blocks apart and had no visual connection. Most of Bloomsbury's squares were larger than those in the South End.

Today, with its seemingly endless blocks of nineteenth-century row houses relieved only by the green patches of eight historic squares and a few recently developed parks, the South End is the largest urban Victorian neighborhood in the United States. Although the squares lend character to the neighborhood and help define it, relatively few Bostonians outside of the South End are aware of them, and only in the past few years have tourist maps started to include the South End. Two factors may account for the South End's obscurity: its decades of physical decline, and its location away from the popular downtown area, which includes the Beacon Hill neighborhood and the adjacent Back Bay. Recently, however, the economic revival of the South End has led to a renewed interest in its squares.

Bulfinch's Vision

As Boston prospered in the early nineteenth century, Charles Bulfinch, having completed Franklin Place in 1795, laid out a large garden square—Columbia Square—as the centerpiece of a grid plan for a still-undeveloped strip of land connecting the mainland with the Shawmut Peninsula. This was a bold step for the town's chief administrator, for until this time Franklin Place—privately developed and financially unsuccessful—had been Boston's only garden square. The new square was named after the ship *Columbia*, the first American ship to circumnavigate the globe. *Columbia*'s voyages had been partially funded by the Bulfinch family from 1787 to 1800. In 1801, Bulfinch predicted that this area, located about one mile south of the downtown business district, would be the next fashionable residential neighborhood in Boston. Eventually his vision was realized—albeit for only two decades during the middle of the nineteenth century. By that time the Neck had been filled in to its present size of one square mile and had become known as the South End.

While he was working on private architectural commissions as well as on Franklin Place, his own speculative real estate venture, Bulfinch had been elected to Boston's Board of Selectmen, where he served from 1791 to 1795. In 1799 he was elected chairman (or chief administrator), an unpaid position he was to hold for eighteen years in a town whose population doubled between 1797 and 1817. Bulfinch's responsibilities included overseeing the planning and construction of new and wider streets as well as new public buildings, wharves, and bridges; the draining and filling of marshlands; the cutting down of hills; and the extension of street lighting, sewers, and water pipes. In addition to these municipal improvements during Bulfinch's tenure, in 1803 a law had been enacted in Boston requiring the use of brick or stone for all public and large private buildings. Similar in many respects to London's Building Act of 1774, this law was to have a great impact on the subsequent appearance of Boston.

As chairman of the Board of Selectmen, Bulfinch focused on improving the infrastructure of the more populous parts of Boston near downtown. Yet, with residential space downtown becoming scarce, he also foresaw that it would soon be necessary to fill in and occupy the Neck to the south. At a town meeting in 1801, he presented an innovative "Plan of the Land on the Neck." The plan, as reported in the March 16, 1801, *Boston Gazette*, described the future layout of the area as follows:

> The streets are regular and drawn at right angles, and to introduce variety, a large circular place is left to be ornamented with trees, which will add to the beauty of the town at large, and be particularly advantageous to the inhabitants of this part. Should the town not think it advisable to fill these lands at present, the Selectmen would still recommend that the streets be laid out according to the plan proposed.

When Bulfinch drew up his plan for the Neck, it was the first time that a representative of the town had taken the initiative in planning a residential district in Boston. It was not until the 1820s that the city would begin to play a significant role in planning under the direction of Mayor Josiah Quincy. By recommending the commitment of town resources to laying out a large public garden for future residents of the area, Bulfinch was suggesting an urban landscape form that, although traditionally predicated on private ownership, he had already used in his own Franklin Place, with its tiny garden. This was the third time that he had proposed the creation of a garden square as an important component of a residential development. In addition to Franklin Place, his 1796 plan for the Mount Vernon Proprietors had also featured a garden space. In the South End, without the space limitations of the downtown area, Bulfinch was able to propose an ample, five-acre "circular" garden—called Columbia Square—that was almost identical in size and shape to London's oval-shaped Bedford Square (one of the Bloomsbury squares). The difference was that Columbia Square was to be divided into equal halves by Washington Street, which meant that the garden would always be visible to the many people who traveled on this major thoroughfare.

It is interesting that Bulfinch chose for the garden a rounded shape inserted into a rectangle. Perhaps he was determined to insert his artistic flourish into an unimaginative but practical grid plan. The large, rectangular blocks may have been intended as sites for attached houses, for in 1801, Bulfinch was at work on the design for Park Row, a group of four large, attached mansions downtown on Park Street. Unfortunately his plan for the Neck was not immediately successful in attracting a large number of residents to the area, and he would never see his vision fully realized. Appointed Architect of the Capitol by President Monroe in 1817, Bulfinch moved to Washington and did not return to Boston until 1829. Retired, he remained in Boston until his death in 1844 at the age of eighty-one.

When lots in the vicinity of Columbia Square were sold, the garden turned out to be the primary attraction, just as Bulfinch had intended. In 1802, the town auctioned sixteen house lots near the square at a cost averaging twelve-and-a-half cents per square foot. The Hales map (1814), the first Boston map to show all existing buildings, depicted Columbia Square as a tree-lined oval bisected by Washington Street, with a few dwellings dotting Washington Street but none in any other location on the grid. In 1825, two lots were sold for thirty-three-and-a-half cents per square foot, a significant increase in price. In 1826, the Boston City Council's Committee on Neck Lands was authorized to sell up to twenty-five additional lots on either side of Washington Street.

In October 1825, encouraged by the rising values of house lots near Columbia Square and motivated by the prospect of raising revenue by making additional lots available for sale, the city reconfigured Bulfinch's grid plan. Since row houses were already becoming the dominant style of housing in the increasingly congested downtown area, the city decided that narrower rectangular blocks would be more suitable for row houses. According to the new plan drawn by city surveyor S. P. Fuller, who had also drawn up the plan for Louisburg Square in 1826, the streets running parallel to Washington Street on each side were drawn two hundred feet apart, as compared to the three hundred feet shown on the original plan. This new configuration, designed to accommodate two rows of attached houses separated by an alley, reduced the size of Columbia Square by one hundred feet at the ends parallel to Washington Street.

When they learned of the new plan for the Neck Lands, Joseph Field, a Boston selectman, and several neighbors petitioned the Committee on Neck Lands in March 1826, stating that they were among those who, in 1802, had purchased house lots either bordering on the square or situated near it. In about 1805, Field had built a large, freestanding brick house at the corner of Washington and East Concord streets. According to the petitioners, their deeds stipulated that the "circular place would always be kept open to its original extent," and if this new plan were implemented, the conditions and stipulations made in the deeds would be violated. They further indicated that they had paid a premium for their lots because of the nearby garden, which they referred to as both the "mall" and the "public square." By stating that "this circular place was fenced and trees were set out at the northwest side and in other parts," Field's petition confirmed the accuracy of the depiction of Columbia Square on the 1814 Hales map.

As a result of Field's petition, the City Council ordered Fuller to draw up another plan, this time retaining the original depth of the garden on either side of Washington Street while keeping the other proposed rectangular blocks that did not affect the size of the garden. Although the 1828 plan still shows the garden with rounded ends, the sides were straight.

By 1828, the city considered Columbia Square as two squares, each with a different name. The square on the east side of Washington Street was named Shawmut Square from 1828 to 1849 (with a brief interlude as Franklin Square from 1845 to 1847), after which it was permanently called Franklin Square. In 1832, the square on the west side was renamed Blackstone Square after William Blackstone, Boston's first English settler.

During the twenty years after Fuller's plan was reworked, the city continued its efforts to sell off property in the vicinity of the two squares. In 1834, the city reaffirmed its commitment to keeping the squares open "for public convenience and ornament forever" by passing an ordinance committing itself to the "care and management of these public lands." An 1836 plan shows the two gardens as being entirely square, without any rounded ends, each with the words "Public Square to remain open for public convenience and ornament forever" inscribed within its perimeter. In 1837, the Boston Land

Co., acting on behalf of the city, put up for auction about a hundred lots in the South End, including eight on Suffolk Street (now Shawmut Avenue) overlooking Blackstone Square. Ten years later, four lots fronting on Blackstone Square were advertised for auction by the city as "a delightful situation for elegant dwelling houses."

The city continued to appreciate the importance of the garden Bulfinch had placed on his 1801 Plan of the Neck, for the reasons he had intended. After all, in 1801 his purpose in laying out Columbia Square was not only "to add to the beauty of the town at large" but also to attract residents to this still-undeveloped part of Boston. Although Bulfinch's third garden square was not an immediate financial success, the city understood its potential value as an amenity that would attract buyers. Since all three downtown squares, which were much smaller than Columbia Square, had become desirable addresses by the 1840s, it was not inconceivable that one or more garden squares in the new South End could become just as prestigious. The concept of the garden square, no longer new to Boston as it had been when Bulfinch began Franklin Place in 1793, offered a potential solution to the city's growing economic problems.

Squares as a Planning Tool

By the 1840s, the Industrial Revolution had dramatically transformed the port city of Boston. Its maritime economy had evolved into a manufacturing economy supported by the newly introduced railroad, new industries, and a new class of citizens—factory workers. The potato famines in Ireland during the 1840s had resulted in a great influx of unskilled Irish laborers, who soon found work in the new ironworks and in the textile and shoe factories. Fueled by old merchant capital and a rapidly expanding labor force, the city prospered, its population doubling (to 137,000) between 1830 and 1850.

Although the steam railroad had been introduced to Boston in 1835, residents seeking transportation within the city still relied almost entirely on horses. But the vehicles for local transportation evolved from private horses and carriages to the public omnibuses introduced in 1826 and then to the horsecar railway (or "street railway," as it was often called) introduced in 1852. This evolution was to have a great effect on where Boston's residents chose to live. While some would choose to take advantage of transportation improvements to live within the city proper, others would see these improvements as an opportunity to move farther out from the city.

Letters written between 1851 and 1859 by South End residents Otis Everett, Jr., and his wife Elizabeth to their son Otis, who worked as a merchant in India, provide a unique, firsthand glimpse of life in the South End during the period. The Everetts lived in a wood, Federal-style house (considered "old-fashioned" by Mrs. Everett), which was built in the late 1790s on Washington Street at the corner of Blake's Court. A letter written in 1856 by Mrs. Everett reveals that South End residents had strong views about the latest transportation improvements affecting their neighborhood:

> A sharp and noisy contest is now going on in the city between those *for* and *against* the Washington Street railroad. The South Enders are about equally divided, one party being sure it will ruin the value of all South End property, and the other party that it will raise the value a hundred percent.

Boston's increased wealth and mobility resulted in an expanded middle class committed to hard work and thrift and wishing to purchase their own homes. Since land in the downtown area was either no longer available or too expensive, many began to look beyond the peninsula for housing. Middle-class residents began to move to the three nearby towns of Roxbury, West Roxbury, and Dorchester even before these towns began to be serviced by the street railways in 1856. The Everett letters contain several references to visits they made to friends and relatives living in Roxbury and Dorchester in 1856. By the mid-nineteenth century, faced with the responsibility of continuing to improve the city's infrastructure in order to keep up with the demands of its increasing population, the municipal government was anxious to expand its tax base. Finding a way to retain the hundreds of people who were leaving Boston for the suburbs was the best solution to this problem.

In 1846, the city launched an ambitious urban-planning project for the Neck Lands, which had already expanded significantly through landfill operations from the area laid out on Bulfinch's 1801 plan. By 1852, the Neck Lands would encompass a 240-acre district bounded by Dover Street to the north, Northampton Street to the south, just beyond Tremont Street to the west, and the South Bay to the east. Because the Neck Lands were low lying and marshy, the project entailed major filling and grading operations as well as the construction of sewers, drains, and streets to make the land both sanitary and marketable. To prevent flooding, the streets were graded fifteen feet above the low-water mark, and the building sites were ten to fifteen feet below street level. This solution to the potential problem of street flooding ultimately resulted in houses whose first floors were accessed by several or more steps above street level, and whose basements (sometimes referred to as ground floors) were several steps below street level in the front but on-grade with the rear alleys. This construction technique, which the city found attractive because it entailed less filling, was identical to the method used for eighteenth-century London terrace houses.

In 1848, Josiah Quincy, Jr., chairman of the City Council's Joint Standing Committee on Public Lands, commissioned Ezra Lincoln, Jr., a civil engineer, to draw up a new plan of city lands and streets southwest of Dover Street. The purpose of this plan was to enable prospective buyers to learn the elevation of the new streets and drains as well as the location of all house lots. Quincy stated, "The filling of these flats will add at the same time greatly to the health and beauty of the city, and by increasing its limits, will retain those who would be driven from it for want of room." The 1848 plan depicts Blackstone and Franklin squares in great detail as they then existed, with paths leading to a small central circle—probably not yet a fountain—and trees bordering four grass plats in each square as well as each square's entire perimeter. In his inaugural address of January 1, 1849, Mayor John Prescott Bigelow urged that "every practicable method be adopted to bring these lands into market. If judiciously managed they will go far towards defraying the public debt."

Although it is not known exactly whose idea it was to create additional squares, as early as 1850 the Joint Committee on Public Lands had been authorized to lay out new streets and sewers in addition to "squares on the public lands." It is obvious that the city, having realized that Blackstone and Franklin squares had proved relatively successful in attracting buyers to their immediate neighborhood, was determined to try to replicate Bulfinch's vision by laying out garden squares in other undeveloped areas of the Neck Lands. Considering garden squares an integral part of its new infrastructure, the city undertook the design of three new squares—Chester Square, Union Park, and Worcester Square—while at the same time taking the opportunity to embellish its two older squares, Blackstone and Franklin. Almost fifty years after the creation of Columbia Square, however, the city was not willing to devote as much space to the garden squares as Bulfinch had in his original plan for the Neck. The three new squares, substantially smaller than either Blackstone or Franklin, were inserted into sections of streets already shown on the plan. The proposed house lots for these squares were stepped back from the street line to create wider spaces with curved or bowed ends.

Between 1846 and 1853, the Joint Committee on Public Lands could boast the following infrastructure improvements:

> Nearly five miles of streets have been filled up and graded—common sewers have been laid therein—sidewalks have been made and edge stones put down in a large portion of them. Five public squares [Blackstone, Franklin, and the three new ones] have been laid out and enclosed with iron fences, and in other respects rendered pleasant and

attractive places of resort. Seven stone fountains [the stone basins that collected water] have been completed, about 1,000 trees have been set out, and 3,000 feet of sea wall have been constructed. These extensive and important improvements have been conducted at an expenditure of $504,290.

Believing that beautiful gardens would entice individual buyers and real estate speculators, the city felt pressure to complete its garden squares as quickly as possible. In fact, part of the auction plan for Chester Square was the city's commitment to improve Chester Square and Chester Street with trees, fences, and walkways before January 1852. As a result, the gardens in the South End squares were completed while the city attempted to sell the lots around them, but well before the onset of any appreciable new home construction. In this respect the new squares differed from two of Boston's earlier, privately developed squares—Louisburg and Pemberton—where the new house owners, according to their deeds, were charged with the responsibility of embellishing and caring for their central garden spaces.

Although the developed gardens might have increased the value of the surrounding lots, sales did not go as well as expected. And even when the lots sold, especially to speculators, buildings did not go up immediately. As early as 1852, the Joint Committee on Public Lands proposed offering incentives to any purchaser who erected a building within a specified time period. This proposal was not adopted until several years later. Even though the committee noted in 1853 that demand for lots was increasing, by 1855, Mayor J. V. C. Smith reported that almost no public lands had been sold during the previous year. Smith recommended that prices be lowered to attract "mechanics of limited means," for speculators were buying up the land for future profits and were not building houses. Describing the Neck Lands as a "region of forsaken nakedness," he also suggested insisting that buildings be erected within reasonable time periods.

An 1852 map of Boston by Slatter and Callan shows that the city, in order to stimulate sales, had placed its three newest squares (Chester and Worcester squares, and Union Park) in areas where there were no dwellings at all. The map depicts in some detail the layout of the gardens and confirms information in city records indicating that by this time (1852) the city had completed the gardens in the three new squares, even though the house lots in Worcester Square would not be auctioned until 1859. The map also reveals that in 1852, Chester Square and Union Park were devoid of houses—as they would be for several more years, even though many house lots in both squares had already been sold.

Although the city planned its three new squares simultaneously, they were developed at different rates, with each square soon taking

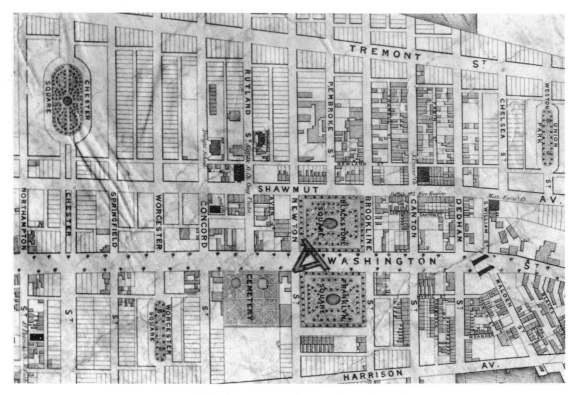

on a life of its own. The timeline for each square affected the architectural style of its dwellings, the design of its garden, and the nature
of its residents. Blackstone and Franklin squares were completed several years before the others. It is instructive to compare the houses,
gardens, and residents of all five squares.

Blackstone and Franklin Squares

The two earliest squares, Blackstone and Franklin, were by far the
city's largest squares, with each garden measuring about 355 feet by
300 feet (or two-and-a-half acres). They were laid out in 1801 —
almost fifty years before the other South End squares. During the
intervening fifty years the city was to gain a better understanding of
the important role that garden squares could play in real estate development and what the city needed to do to protect and maintain the
gardens. But right from the beginning, the city was committed to
keeping Blackstone and Franklin squares open forever for "convenience and ornament." It understood that these gardens—as long as
they were attractive—were valuable assets and that people would
be willing to pay a premium to live near them. Over time, as both
developer and owner of the public gardens, the city discovered that

there was a definite correlation between the timing of heightened landscaping activity and the sporadic bursts of housing construction in the squares.

The dwellings built in Blackstone and Franklin squares represented an unusually wide variety of architectural styles because some houses already existed in these squares by 1850 when the city laid out additional squares. The 1848 plan of the South End indicates that at least six of the eight lots that had been put up for auction in 1837 along Suffolk Street (now Shawmut Avenue) overlooking the garden in Blackstone Square had been sold. It is also known that six row houses were built on these lots between 1845 and 1847. These houses were similar in style to the brick bowfronts of Louisburg Square, most of which had been built between 1830 and 1840. With their pedimented entrances, plain, flush lintels, taller parlor windows on the first floor, cast-iron decorative balconies, and granite steps, these houses represented late examples of the Greek Revival style in Boston. In 1847, two of the houses were still vacant, but the others were occupied by a mason, a lawyer, an iron manufacturer, and a member of the clergy—primarily middle-class residents who were not as prominent as those attracted to Louisburg Square. Because of their relatively plain style, these houses were reasonably priced at about $6,000.

By 1847, when Blackstone Square finally had several dwellings, the city thought that it was time to honor its commitment to keep the gardens for "public convenience and ornament." This may have been when the city established the landscape design that remains to this day. The 1848 plan shows diagonal paths and four semicircular grass plats edged by trees in each of the two squares, as well as an additional row of street trees around the perimeter of each square. Nevertheless, the newly improved landscapes must not have satisfied the residents and property owners, who may have had higher standards than the city regarding the appearance of the gardens. According to Nathaniel Shurtleff in *A Topographical and Historical Description of Boston*, new iron fences were installed in Blackstone and Franklin squares in 1849. The *1852 Boston Almanac* noted that the residents and property owners in these two squares had contributed about half of the total cost (or $4,000 out of $10,000) of two thirteen-hundred-foot iron fences. To reach an agreement with the city concerning who would pay for what, the residents or their representatives must have had to spend a substantial amount of time negotiating with city officials.

The fence the city installed was not identical to the one in Louisburg Square, although the city ultimately chose the lotus-stalk fence for its three new squares. Rather, the fence was identical to the one

Franklin Square, in a
stereocard view by John
S. Moulton, ca. 1870s.
Stereocard. Boston Athenæum.

The fences in Blackstone and
Franklin squares, having been
installed several years earlier
than the fences in the South
End's next three squares, were
of a different design. The use
of bollards at the entrances to
the gardens is more welcoming
than the more traditional gates,
which could be locked to
restrict access to the gardens.

surrounding the Church of the Immaculate Conception, which was
later built nearby on Harrison Avenue in 1861. The style of fence
used around the gardens of Blackstone and Franklin squares appears
to have been more elaborate and a half-foot taller than the one in
Louisburg Square (which cost $2,264 for 535 feet plus four lamp-
posts), yet it actually cost about the same amount per linear foot
as the Louisburg Square fence. The residents must have felt a sense
of satisfaction that theirs was a more impressive-looking fence—
whether or not they had played a role in selecting it.

The next significant development in the squares occurred at the
northeast corner of Franklin Square. Although ownership of the property had changed several times since 1828, no dwellings had been
built. The original property was a square shape and probably was
intended for a freestanding house, possibly oriented toward the garden, with its side facing Washington Street. As row houses grew in
popularity, it became obvious that building several houses facing the
garden would be much more lucrative. In 1850, Gardner Chilson, a
Boston merchant whose company sold stoves and hot-air furnaces,
entered into a speculative real estate venture with Russell Sturgis, a
London merchant. (Chilson lived at 1 Chilson Place in Boston's West
End.) Upon selling his Brookline Street property to Chilson for $1.82
per square foot—a very high price for South End land, which at the
time was selling for well under $1.00 per square foot—Sturgis agreed
to refund one-third of the selling price if Chilson erected at least four
dwelling houses within a year. Having spent a total of $12,500 for the
property, Chilson built four dwellings in the course of the next
year—and had no trouble selling them almost immediately to several
other Boston merchants for at least $20,000 each.

These majestic row houses, each topped with an Italianate-style cupola (often described in contemporary accounts as an "octagonal observatory"), must have been quite imposing as they loomed high above the nearby gardens. Even the lot frontages of the two end houses—thirty-six feet for the corner house and thirty-two feet for the last house of the row—were wider than usual. In letters written to her son in 1855 and 1856, Mrs. Everett refers to these impressive dwellings as "the Chilson houses" and notes that Timothy Sumner, a merchant who had bought 4 East Brookline Street in 1852, had "furnished it splendidly."

On November 15, 1851, *Gleason's Pictorial Drawing-Room Companion* published an engraving of the "four spacious mansions fronting Franklin Square" and described the particular architectural features that gave these Italianate row houses "an air of great beauty and completeness." The presence of so many hallmarks of the Italianate style —bold forms and elaborate ornament—distinguished these houses from their Greek Revival companions in Blackstone Square as well as their predecessors in the downtown area during the 1830s and 1840s. Unique to these four new houses was the equal balance between brick and brownstone, with the brownstone used for the rusticated

Corner of Washington and East Brookline (Franklin Square), in a photograph by Josiah Hawes, ca. 1860. Courtesy of the Boston Public Library, Print Department.

This photograph shows the four attached Chilson Houses in Franklin Square at the corner of Washington and East Brookline streets. The wooden frames supporting the young elms, planted about thirty feet apart along Washington Street between Blackstone and Franklin squares, demonstrate the city's early sophistication in tree care.

basements, the quoins at the corners, the trim along the four sides of each window, and a heavy cornice and small balcony projecting over each entrance.

Unusual for Boston at the time were the impressive scale and architectural features of these Italianate row houses, features that were rarely replicated to this extent in any later South End row houses. Chilson spared no expense in developing this prime property, which was not only situated along an omnibus route but also fronted on two attractive gardens. Even *Gleason's Pictorial Drawing-Room Companion* acknowledged that "the fine trees that ornament the neighborhood, and the spacious airy beauty of Franklin and Blackstone squares have attracted the attention of persons who desire choice building lots and a fine location."

By 1851 when Chilson's houses were completed and occupied, the city had already begun to make further improvements to the gardens of Blackstone and Franklin squares while simultaneously beginning to work on the gardens in its three new squares. The 1849 fences already needed painting, and the city apparently covered this expense. However, city records show that the abutters were required to pay $500 of the $1,500 cost to erect a light fence around the fountains, paint the fountain vases, remove dead trees, and plant additional trees. This was the second time that the residents of Blackstone and Franklin squares had agreed to share expenses with the city for improvements to the gardens. In this early public/private partnership, not only had the residents funded capital improvements such as new fences, they now were willing to fund such maintenance tasks as painting the fountain vases and planting new trees.

Even though it required frequent painting, cast iron was often used for ornamental purposes—for instance, in fences, balconies, and fountains—starting in the late 1840s. Less expensive than wrought iron, cast iron could be produced by large foundries in bulk and sold through catalogs or pattern books. Both speculative builders and municipalities quickly understood that mass-produced ornaments for houses and gardens would appeal to representatives of the middle classes who were anxious to display their new wealth. The Chilson houses and the brownstone row on West Newton Street in Blackstone Square had graceful iron-scroll railings, low iron fences protecting the areas in front of their basement windows, and, along the roofs, iron cresting that served as a decorative snow guard.

Although most commonly painted black, fences were sometimes painted dark green, particularly in London until the death of Queen Victoria's husband, Prince Albert, in 1861, after which black was used as a sign of mourning. Green recently was found to be the original paint color for a front-yard fence in Union Park, but it is difficult to

Stereograph of Blackstone
Square, 1860s.
Private collection.

This stereograph shows a man standing under the *allée* of elms planted
twenty feet apart along one of the four diagonal paths leading to the
fountain in Blackstone Square. The young trees have not yet begun to
exhibit the umbrella-shaped branching that made elms the popular
choice for all urban plantings of the period.

tell from early photographs whether the fence enclosing the central garden in any of the squares was originally green. Even though fountains were usually painted black, the fountains in three of the squares —Chester Square, Union Park, and Worcester Square—were painted white to resemble stone, which was perceived to be a more sophisticated material than the ubiquitous cast iron.

In its effort to attract prospective buyers, the city lost no time in ornamenting its public squares with fashionable cast-iron fountains that could take advantage of Boston's new water supply from Lake Cochituate in Natick, about fifteen miles west of the city. In his 1849 inaugural address as mayor of Boston, John Prescott Bigelow had remarked, "The City, at last, enjoys the long-coveted blessing—a copious supply of Pure Water." Although there were costs associated with using the new water supply (as was shown in the discussion of Louisburg Square's fountain), the city did not seem to mind paying for water consumed by the fountains in its public squares.

In its Report to the City Council of Boston in 1852, the Cochituate Water Board listed ten public fountains supplied with Cochituate water. Of these ten, three were located in South End squares—one each in Blackstone and Franklin squares and one in Chester Square. According to this report, the fountains in Blackstone and Franklin squares were "of cast iron in the shape of an ornamental vase supported on a fluted column." (It is likely that the report was referring to a fluted vase on an ornamental column decorated with four dolphins.) The top of the vase was seven feet nine inches above the forty-five-foot-diameter basin, and three jets sprayed water up to seven feet above the vase. *The Boston Almanac for the Year 1852* notes that a "Cochituate fountain was provided in the center of each square, at a cost of $750 each, exclusive of the pipe and vase." This expense, which may have referred to the columns adorned with dolphins, might have been covered by the residents, who could have selected and ordered the columns from a catalog. The new occupants of the "Chilson houses," in particular, would surely have wanted Franklin Square's garden to look as fine—or even finer—than the gardens in the downtown squares.

The improvements to the gardens in Blackstone and Franklin squares may have spurred construction activity. Although the previously mentioned 1848 plan indicates that five lots had been sold in Blackstone Square on West Brookline Street at the corner of Shawmut, houses were not built on most of them until several years later. The attached buildings that were eventually constructed included a large, brick Greek Revival house with granite steps and a pedimented entrance, and a very elaborate brownstone house built by Nathaniel Winsor in 1853 as a replacement for an earlier dwelling on the site.

Winsor, Jr., was a prosperous downtown Boston merchant who owned a large fleet of packet ships. At the southeast end of Franklin Square, separated from the garden by a street running between East Newton and East Brookline streets, there was another large, rectangular property, on which eight row houses were erected by 1852. These houses may have been unremarkable, for photographs of this side of the square have not been found.

An impressive row of twelve Italianate flat-front brownstones was soon erected on West Newton Street overlooking the garden in Blackstone Square. Although nine of them were built at different times between 1851 and 1855, they were identical in appearance. The frontage of each house measured the standard twenty-five feet, yet the houses were unusually tall because they had four rather than three full stories in addition to a basement and an attic with servants' bedrooms. The use of brownstone for the entire flat façade, which extended the length of the block, not only was rare for residential architecture in Boston but also resulted in an imposing, if mono-

Blackstone Square, West Newton Street, 1855. Courtesy of the Society for the Preservation of New England Antiquities.

This stereograph shows nine Italianate brownstone houses on West Newton Street facing the garden of Blackstone Square. The earlier, red-brick Federal-style houses at the corner of Washington Street were later replaced by three matching brownstones.

chromatic, group of houses that captured the attention of the public. All the traditional Italianate features, which required a malleable stone, also were executed in brownstone—fluted Doric pilasters supporting horizontal entablatures around the double doorways, windows surmounted by bracketed lintels, and paired brackets supporting a prominent cornice at the roofline. The September 1, 1855, *Ballou's Pictorial Drawing-Room Companion* compared these elegant row houses to the new buildings going up in New York City, where four- to six-inch-thick brownstone slabs applied over brick had become the material of choice for those seeking sophisticated luxury housing.

The only remaining side of Franklin Square—the East Newton Street block—was never the site of row houses. Instead, Jonas Chickering, an internationally known piano manufacturer, acquired a large piece of property facing the square in 1837. By 1852, Chickering and his partner John Mackay had built a large piano warehouse on the site. Shortly thereafter the building was sold to Hamblen and Brown, who leased it to Silas and Ira Warren. This transaction provoked Mrs. Everett, who in 1855 wrote the following to her son: "The neighbors on Franklin Square are all in an uproar because Warren, the Police man, has hired Chickering's large building, on the side next the burying ground, and intends fitting it up to let out to Irish." Their fears were not realized. The building was replaced by a piano factory, which was destroyed by fire in 1864. The property was then sold to Maturin Ballou, editor of *Ballou's Pictorial Drawing-Room Companion*, who built the St. James Hotel on the site—in the French Second Empire style—in 1868.

By 1855, Blackstone and Franklin squares had become fashionable enclaves where the scale of the buildings and gardens was grander than the scale of any of the more cramped downtown squares. The Shawmut Congregational Church, constructed in 1851 and located a block away from Blackstone Square on Shawmut Avenue, was an amenity for residents of the new neighborhood just as the Boston Theatre and Holy Cross Church had been for residents of Bulfinch's Franklin Place. (Although Bulfinch's houses in Franklin Place were of the highest style, by 1858 they were about to be demolished.) Compared to the two Italianate rows in Blackstone and Franklin squares, the Greek Revival row houses of Louisburg and Pemberton squares were quite ordinary.

In fulfilling its commitment to embellish the gardens of Blackstone and Franklin squares, the city was able to accomplish its goal of attracting builders who would erect fashionable dwellings that middle-class residents would then buy. The residents attracted by the houses overlooking the expansive gardens were not from Boston's mercan-

tile families, who had made their money at the end of the eighteenth and in the beginning of the nineteenth centuries. Instead, most represented the upper-middle-class manufacturers of leather boots and shoes, and newly available household goods, who were prospering in Boston as a result of the Industrial Revolution.

In 1855, *Ballou's Pictorial Drawing-Room Companion* noted that garden squares such as Blackstone Square served two functions, as "breathing holes" that contributed to "public health and comfort," and as "ornaments to the localities where they are placed." It is obvious that for fifty years the city's motivation in embellishing Blackstone and Franklin squares had been exclusively as a lure for potential

Stereograph of Blackstone Square, early 1860s. Courtesy of David R. Hocker.

This view of Blackstone Square is toward the corner of West Brookline Street and Shawmut Avenue. Two women wearing the latest Victorian fashions are promenading around the fountain. The steeple of the First Shawmut Congregational Church is visible in the background.

Blackstone Square, Boston.
Ballou's Pictorial Drawing-Room Companion, August 11, 1855.
Private collection.

This engraving of Blackstone Square depicts Washington Street in the foreground as a bustling thoroughfare for carriages and omnibuses in the period just before the horsecar railway was introduced to the South End. In the background are the Italianate brownstones on West Newton Street and the Greek Revival row houses on Shawmut Avenue.

development rather than for any health benefits that might accrue to its citizens.

Chester Square

In choosing to keep Blackstone and Franklin squares as open gardens for so many years, the city was continuing the tradition of Charles Bulfinch. But in creating three new garden squares—Chester Square, Union Park, and Worcester Square—the city did more than continue a tradition. It exhibited a growing confidence that its investment in additional squares would pay off.

Chester Square, located in a less-convenient area at the southern edge of the South End, was inserted into the 75-foot-wide Chester Street, the South End's second broadest street after the 100-foot-wide Washington Street. Its garden, which had straight sides and curved ends, measured 400 feet by 164 feet, contained an acre and a half, and would be the largest of the three new gardens (consequently, it required the greatest investment of city funds). By pushing back the house lots from the street line to allow for a broader garden, the city had to give up a total of thirty-two lots—with their potential revenues. Sixteen of these lots would normally have backed onto an alley and fronted on Springfield Street north of the square; the other sixteen would have fronted on Northampton Street to the south. In a newly fashionable neighborhood, higher values usually were associated with garden frontage. However, the increased income from both the sale of the deeper house lots extending from Chester Square to Springfield and Northampton streets and, later, the houses built on them, was expected to more than make up for the initial loss in revenue.

The city's vision for Chester Street went beyond simply creating a large garden that would be easily visible only to the residents whose houses lined its perimeter. The 1850 plan for Chester Square includes a twenty-foot-wide mall beginning at both ends of the garden and extending almost two hundred feet in both directions to Tremont Street and Suffolk Street (now Shawmut Avenue), as well as one block farther south beyond Suffolk to Washington Street, the South

Stereograph of Chester Park, late 1850s.
Courtesy of The Bostonian Society/ Old State House.

This stereograph shows the mall in front of 27 Chester Park, which was located between the garden of Chester Square and Shawmut Avenue, looking west toward Chester Square and its fountain. The city planted this early mall with a double row of elm trees and enclosed it with a simple but decorative iron fence.

End's main thoroughfare. Chester Street was renamed Chester Park in June of 1858, and later that year the block between Tremont and Suffolk streets was officially named Chester Square. In 1864, the additional segment of Chester Park between Suffolk and Washington streets was also named Chester Square. Ultimately the extensions of the mall beyond Washington and Tremont streets were called, respectively, East Chester Park and West Chester Park. This fenced-in mall with grass and a double row of trees pre-dated by almost ten years the well-known, hundred-foot-wide mall on Commonwealth Avenue in the Back Bay. The city hoped it would become a fashionable boulevard that would attract more residents to the neighborhood.

In an effort to make the Chester Square lots as desirable as possible, the city promised (on its Plan for City Lands to be sold on October 30, 1850) to improve Chester Square and Chester Street with trees, fences, and walks by January 1852. According to the *Boston Daily Evening Transcript*, between two hundred and three hundred people turned out for the Chester Square auction, but only about half of the ninety lots facing the garden and mall between Tremont and Washington streets were sold. Most of these went to about twenty-five speculative builders, few of whom bought more than two or three adjoining lots. These builders paid as much as one dollar per square foot for lots close to Washington Street; about the same amount for lots on the north side of the square (which was closer to downtown), and around eighty-five cents per square foot for lots on the south side. At the time of the auction the garden had not yet been completed, so these prices reflected the speculators' greater interest in lots that were closer to Washington Street as well as to downtown.

After the auction the city immediately began to honor its commitment to Chester Square. In June 1851, the city listed expenses for the following improvements: labor and material for filling Chester Street and Chester Square; fencing and ornaments for Chester Square, including the fountain; laying the remaining edge stones (curbing); paving sidewalks; and furnishing and setting trees. Although the 1850 auction plan depicts a simple layout of four straight paths leading to a central fountain, an undated drawing shows the addition of four primary curved paths that create curvilinear quadrants with narrower curved paths. We know this version of the design was implemented, for it was shown on the 1852 Slatter and Callan Map of the City of Boston.

Both the 1850 plan and the 1852 map depict trees lining all paths as well as the perimeter of the garden. According to the *1852 Boston Almanac*, Chester Square had a 987-foot iron fence, which cost four thousand dollars, and a fountain, which cost a thousand dollars. Unlike in Blackstone and Franklin squares, the city had no choice but to

Stereograph of Chester Square, ca. 1859.
Courtesy of David R. Hocker.

cover the entire cost of these furnishings since there were as yet no residents. The fence was identical to the lotus-stalk fence in Louisburg Square—with gas lanterns extending from some of the pickets —and cost about the same amount per linear foot. The three-tiered cast-iron fountain topped by a small, two-handled urn, was almost identical to a fountain shown in the 1859 Chase Brothers & Co. catalog as well as the 1870 Janes, Kirtland & Co. catalog. (The former company was located in Boston; the latter was a New York company, which started out making furnaces in 1845 and added ornamental ironwork in the early 1850s.) The fountain's large basin was fifty feet in diameter, only five feet wider than the fountain basins in Blackstone and Franklin squares. According to the 1852 annual report of

This stereograph of Chester Square shows the same lotus-stalk fence (with one lantern) as was used to enclose the garden in Louisburg Square. The only difference is that Chester Square's fence had four double gates whereas Louisburg Square's fence did not include a gate until the twentieth century.

the Cochituate Water Board, which kept detailed records on water consumption, the Chester Square fountain with two jets used a total of 56,000 gallons of water. The fountains in Blackstone and Franklin squares, with three jets each, used 64,000 gallons apiece.

Most of the dwellings in Chester Square were built and sold between 1855 and 1859, with only three or four lots still vacant in 1859. Even with the attraction of a large garden, however, the builders must not have felt as confident as the builders in Blackstone and Franklin squares, where many of the early dwellings had brownstone façades. Of the forty houses fronting directly on the garden in Chester Square, only five were built with brownstone fronts, and these five commanded a higher selling price than their brick counterparts.

The Chester Square houses exhibited lavish use of the latest architectural features in both the Italianate and Gothic styles. Heavy bracketed brownstone hoods and lintels, rusticated basements, prominent cornices, arched double doorways, high stoops with brownstone balustrades, and decorative ironwork in the form of areaway fences, scrolled stoop railings, and balconies created a medley of distinctive dwellings that was unusual for row houses. The widespread use of French-style mansard roofs, just coming into fashion in the late 1850s, added an element of verticality to the buildings while also creating a full-story attic. Since all but seven of the Chester Square houses had bow fronts, the effect was one of overall uniformity—despite the variety of decorative features used—broken only by two tall, flat-front brownstones, with cupolas, that served as an architectural keystone at the center of the square's south side. On the north side two pairs of brick bow fronts (including the two center houses) also had cupolas, but these houses did not stand out as much because their façades were constructed of brick.

The houses at each of the square's bows, where the lot areas were several hundred square feet greater than the other lots in the square, offered builders a unique opportunity to create dwellings with wider frontages that could accommodate more elaborate ornamentation and, consequently, sell for a higher price. The buildings at three of the four bows were particularly impressive as they stepped forward, one against the other. Each displayed its richly decorated side bay windows, which commanded a good view of the garden. At the eastern end of the north side, furniture dealer William Carnes, possibly without the assistance of an architect, built two houses that were distinguished by freestanding brownstone porches supported by Corinthian columns, Gothic ornamentation, iron verandas, and billiard rooms on the top floor. One of the houses was sold in 1863 to Axel Dearborn (the owner of a large Boston iron foundry), and the other was occupied by Carnes himself.

Stereograph of Chester
Square, early 1860s.
Courtesy of David R. Hocker.

This view of Chester Square's cast-iron fountain shows that it was
painted white to simulate stone, which would have made it appear
much more elegant. Unlike the basins of Blackstone and Franklin
squares' fountains, the rim of this basin appears to be high enough to
invite sitting. A small bench or stool is visible at the lower right.

The builders of two sets of houses at the western curve of both the north and south sides chose to use architects, which was an unusual practice during this period when most builders served as their own designers. Architect Luther Briggs, Jr., designed the house on the north side (which is now occupied by the South End Historical Society) as well as an adjacent house. Charles O. Rogers, editor and publisher of the *Boston Journal*, commissioned John R. Hall to design the five houses directly across the square from the Briggs houses. In his designs for Charles Rogers, Hall had an opportunity to create luxurious dwellings that contained many custom-designed exterior and interior architectural features as well as some of the more costly items, such as modern plumbing fixtures, represented in catalogs. All of the houses had decorative iron verandas. According to an early deed for the house at 72 Chester Square, which Rogers built for himself in 1858, Hall's plans were implemented by Ivory Bean, a mason, and William Carpenter, a carpenter.

An article in the October 8, 1859, *Boston Saturday Evening Gazette*, which describes in detail Rogers's impressive brick and brownstone house, sheds some light on the interior appointments of a fashionable row house of the period. Although the basic arrangement of the twenty rooms was typical of these row houses, the scale of the rooms and the number of new conveniences—such as thirty closets, five with sinks and some with toilets—were unusual. The basement, which contained a large dining room, had an ell with a kitchen measuring fifteen feet by twenty-two feet. The parlor story, which was accessed by a high stairway, contained a very large drawing room (sixteen feet by forty-two feet) and an oval parlor with thirteen-foot ceilings. Each of the next two floors had two bedrooms, and the top story included a billiard room and three servants' bedrooms. Newly fashionable black walnut was used for the parlor doors as well as the main staircase, in which the railing, decorated with rope moldings and rosettes, extended from the basement all the way up to the billiard room.

Because the house lots in Chester Square were sold to so many different speculators over a period of several years, the houses that were built did not reflect a conscious effort to create a uniform streetscape, as was the case for the block of brownstones fronting on Blackstone Square. The builders had to comply with only a few city requirements, which affected building materials (stone or brick), height (not less than three stories exclusive of basement and attic), setback from the street (uniform), and the use of the structure (as a dwelling house for a minimum of twenty years). To erect dwellings that would be as distinctive as possible, the builders relied heavily on popular pattern books. These builders believed that buyers were willing to pay more for bowfronts than flat fronts, and for elaborate decorative features such as balconies, quoins, and cupolas.

A 1993 study by Margaret Smith and John Moorhouse of nineteenth-century South End row houses confirms that the builders were right. The study concludes that although lot and house size and neighborhood characteristics accounted for 74 percent of the price differential among row houses in the authors' sample, architectural style and features accounted for an additional 14 percent of the cost of these houses. According to the study, buyers were not interested in paying a premium for the more commonplace features, for instance, high stoops with curvilinear iron railings and bracketed hoods over entrances. Another finding was that buyers paid lower prices for dwellings that were part of a long row of identical houses. The Chester Square speculators knew their market well, because only C. O. Rogers & Friends bought more than two or three adjacent lots.

Despite its location in a fairly remote section of the South End, Chester Square was a successful real estate venture largely because the city had committed to constructing a beautiful garden and mall that

The Chester Square residence of Rev. R. C. Waterston, ca. 1860s. Courtesy of the Society for the Preservation of New England Antiquities.

The furnishings in the front parlor, which overlooked the garden, of the Reverend Robert C. Waterston's house at 71 Chester Square reflect the elaborate Victorian style of the period. Portraits of Waterston's wealthy parents by Gilbert Stuart are said to have hung in the house. Mrs. Waterston was a daughter of Mayor Josiah Quincy.

also happened to be close to transportation on Washington Street. In turn, the builders who bought the lots understood precisely what types of dwellings would attract newly successful middle-class buyers. *King's Handbook of Boston*, a local guidebook, referred to the houses as "fine residences, some of them quite elegant and costly." Prospective buyers had a choice of houses in different price ranges—$15,000 for simple brick bowfronts, $21,000 for the center brownstones on the south side, and $28,000 for one of the two lavishly decorated houses built by William Carnes. Accordingly, Chester Square appealed to middle-class residents at a variety of income levels. These residents were primarily merchants in the burgeoning industries of the period —dry goods, shoes, and furniture—men who sat on the boards of banks and other institutions and were anxious to display their new wealth. They were much like the people who had sought to live in Blackstone and Franklin squares, where housing at different prices was also available.

In a letter to her son in 1856, Elizabeth Everett captures the exuberance of life in Chester Square when she notes, "A masquerade ball took place a few evenings ago in the South End at Mr. Lang's in Chester Square, and proved to be a magnificent affair." William Lang was a merchant whose business was located downtown at 31 India Street. After describing the guests' costumes in great detail, Mrs. Everett observes: "There have been so many handsome houses built in the South End that the character of the neighborhood is fast changing from the good old staid nine o'clock customs of my youth, and fashion and style and amusement are now asserting their rights around us."

As early as the middle of 1851, less than a year after the auction of house lots, the Committee on Public Lands seemed to feel the need to justify its promised improvements for Chester Square. By calculating total projected revenues based on the current value of the house lots, the committee concluded that the expenditures for the garden amounted to less than nine cents per square foot. This was certainly a reasonable figure, given that the least-expensive lots on Chester Square had sold for eighty-five cents per square foot and many for as much as one dollar per square foot. Eight years later the remaining unsold lots were selling for three dollars per square foot. Although inflation may have accounted for the increased cost, the large and flourishing garden, which must have been the envy of everyone in Boston, played a major role in raising real estate values around the square.

Local publications waxed eloquent about the many desirable features of Chester Square's garden, including the beautiful fountain (with its basin used as a fish pond, this fountain was a "deliciously

cool and pleasant spot in mid-summer") and the lush assortment of trees, shrubs, and flowers. An article in the December 1926 issue of *Our Boston* contains reminiscences of the garden by the daughter of Captain Howes, one of the early residents of Chester Square. She wrote:

> In summer there was the unusual display of flowers along the borders of the many paths artistically arranged by the dear old gardener. In the winter the scene was again one of pleasure, for the little pond around the fountain was frozen and gave us a most delightful chance to try out the skates Santa Claus brought us.

Although the Chester Square plantings were much more elaborate in design than the simpler grass and trees in Blackstone and Franklin squares, the gardens in all three squares were popular with nursemaids as they tended their young charges.

Stereograph of Chester Square, 1860s.
Private collection.

This stereograph shows the curvilinear paths with borders of grass or groundcover and a naturalistic arrangement of trees and shrubs, all of which combine to give a lush and elegant appearance to Chester Square's garden. The view is from the southwest looking toward the houses on the north side, four of which have cupolas.

Stereograph of Chester Square, early 1860s.
Courtesy of David R. Hocker.

A stylishly dressed woman and several children—one possibly holding a parasol—are seated on benches on one of the pathways in Chester Square's garden, which shows a wide range of plantings. Although most of the plants are not identifiable, the multi-branched shrub with soft round blossoms may be a smokebush.

The city incurred expenses for cutting the grass and taking care of the grounds in Chester Square as early as 1853. However, by 1860, when most of the houses were occupied, the residents must have decided to hire their own private gardener to supplement the city's efforts because the garden exhibited an elaborate selection of flowers, shrubs, and trees. The city might have continued to care for the trees around the perimeter of the garden, but it is doubtful that it would have had the resources to take care of such a large garden. The hiring of a gardener must have been accompanied by a decision to privatize the garden, for access was limited to residents of Chester Square, even though the garden was owned by the city. Many years later Miss Howes recalled, "We who lived in the houses about the enclosure had, as our special privilege, the right to unlock any of the four gates, and go beyond the tall iron fence which marked the boundary for those who had no keys."

In completing Chester Square, which soon became one of Boston's most prestigious addresses, the city had created a garden that, although half the size of either Blackstone or Franklin squares, contained all the traditional features: an iron perimeter fence, a fountain, trees, grass, and benches. In addition, with its curvilinear paths and lush plantings of flowers and shrubs (which the residents may have introduced), the appearance of the garden complemented the highly decorated bowfront dwellings that surrounded the square. The ambiance created by this fashionable horticultural display must have been a source of pride for the residents, who did not hesitate to use the garden for strolling and sitting. The fact that the garden was usually locked meant that it was not as accessible to other South End residents, as the larger Blackstone and Franklin squares were.

Union Park and Worcester Square

In 1850, when selecting locations for two garden squares in addition to Chester Square, the city sought out other areas of the South End that were still undeveloped although not necessarily as remote as Chester Square had been. When planning Chester Square the city had the luxury of a seventy-five-foot-wide street in which to place a large garden, with a mall extending from either end of the garden. The extensive scale of this project was the city's way of compensating for Chester Square's out-of-the-way location. In contrast, the location chosen for Union Park was in an area of the South End that was much closer to downtown; and for Worcester Square, the site was just off Washington Street two blocks south of Franklin Square. Since both squares were superimposed on relatively narrow streets, the area of each garden was one-third of an acre compared to Chester Square's acre and a half. The city hoped that the convenient location of these squares—particularly Union Park—would more than make up for the small size of the gardens, just as it had for the downtown squares many years before.

In laying out its three new squares, the city must have intended to sell the lots in each square immediately in order to reap the financial benefits as soon as possible. Although the city was able to accomplish this goal in Chester Square, things did not run as smoothly in Union Park and Worcester Square. A comparative history of these two squares highlights some of the problems the city faced in developing the South End during the important decade of the 1850s. And just as with all three squares discussed earlier—Blackstone, Franklin, and Chester squares—the length of time the city took to complete the development of a square was to have an impact on both the architectural styles of its dwellings and the nature of the residents.

The city held an auction for the 43 lots directly abutting the garden of Union Park on November 12, 1851—one year after the Chester Square auction. The next day the *Boston Daily Evening Transcript* reported that only 24 of a total of 108 lots in or near Union Park had been sold. According to the article, the cost of the 12 lots directly overlooking the garden ranged from seventy-three cents to eighty-two cents per square foot, whereas the cost of the 12 on Waltham Street one block north of the square brought around sixty-two cents per square foot. Although the results of the auction confirmed that the value of property fronting the garden was higher than that of nearby lots, the city must have been disappointed with the overall lack of interest in its new garden square. To prospective purchasers, Union Park must have seemed rather insubstantial compared to the more remote Chester Square, which not only had deeper lots with a higher value per square foot but also a much larger garden.

The plan for the sale of house lots did not specifically spell out the city's commitment to complete the garden, as the Chester Square plan had. However, the existence of two quite similar plans—one from 1850 and the other undated—meant that the city considered the garden an important attraction for buyers. The 1850 plan shows an oblong garden measuring 320 feet by 50 feet, with rounded ends and two straight paths leading to one central fountain. The path extending the length of the garden was lined with a double row of twelve trees. More trees are drawn along the edge of the sidewalks in front of the house lots. The undated plan is more schematic and does not show trees, but it does picture two fountains rather than one. The 1852 Slatter and Callan map, which accurately depicts the layout of the other South End squares, shows the garden in Union Park with two fountains, a double row of trees, and no paths.

The city had lost no time in doing preliminary work on the garden before the auction. At the end of 1851, the Committee on Public Lands reported expenses for the following Union Park improvements: labor and material for adding fill to Weston Street (the street into which the square had been inserted) and the square; grading, fencing, and fitting up fountains; and furnishing and planting trees. In September 1851, Mrs. Everett wrote to her son, "Union Park is having an iron fence erected round it, and preparations for a fountain, so we shall look in nice order when you return." The same lotus-stalk fence that the city had used for Chester Square's garden was used in Union Park. The *1852 Boston Almanac* noted, "Union Park will soon be liberally ornamented with trees, walks and a Cochituate fountain." Although each of these sources refers to a single fountain, the fact that city records reported expenses for "fitting up fountains" meant that this small square was to have one more fountain than each of the larger squares.

Of particular interest is the fact that the city records probably referred to installing the fountain basins and pumps rather than the actual decorative cast-iron fountains, which may have been added at

Stereograph of Union Park
with a view toward Shaw-
mut Avenue, early 1860s.
Courtesy of David R. Hocker.

A flagpole constructed from a ship's mast towers over Union Park in
this view taken from the Tremont Street end. Twelve elms spaced
about twenty-five feet apart are planted fairly close to the fence on
each side of the garden. A ten-foot-wide walkway bordered by grass
or groundcover extends the length of the garden.

a later date. A stereograph from the 1860s shows two lotus-flower-pattern cast-iron fountain vases in Union Park. Visible at the center of one of the vases—and probably decorating the other fountain vase as well—is an elaborate cast-iron statue of Leda and the Swan, with a water jet spraying into the air from the swan's mouth. The vase and its statue—both painted white like the fountain in Chester Square—are also identical to a stock fountain design shown in the 1870 ironwork catalog from Janes, Kirtland & Co. Pictures of this fountain as well as Chester Square's fountain later appeared in *King's Handbook of Boston* on a page entitled "Monuments and Fountains in Boston."

In 1853, well before all the lots were sold, the city continued its efforts to beautify Union Park's garden in order to attract buyers. The Report of Boston's Superintendent of Public Lands for that year lists expenses not only for furnishing and planting trees but also for watering the trees, cutting the grass, and taking care of the grounds. The completed garden might have helped sales because by 1859—perhaps partly in response to recently introduced financial incentives to build, which were offered by the city—none of the lots were vacant.

Although the frontages of the Union Park lots were only one foot

Fountain pattern for Union Park.

Ornamental Ironwork, Janes, Kirtland & Co. Reprint of 1870 catalog. Private collection.

An 1870 ironwork catalog depicts a statue of Leda and the Swan atop an Egyptian Revival lotus-flower vase that is identical to the two fountains originally installed in Union Park. The height of the fountain and statue together is eight feet. These fountains were originally placed in granite basins, each fifteen feet in diameter.

narrower than their twenty-five-foot counterparts in Chester Square, the end lots beyond the garden were only twenty to twenty-two feet wide. The houses with their ridge rather than mansard roofs were also not as tall as the houses in Chester Square, and their scale was more consistent with the modest size of the central garden space. The first house, built in 1854, was the earliest example of the Greek Revival style represented in Union Park. Most of the other houses contained several traditional Italianate features: rusticated basements, elaborate ironwork front-yard fences and balconies, bracketed hoods with elaborate keystones, and oriels over the hoods on the flat-fronted houses. These features were similar to the ones that decorated the Chester Square houses built during the same period. Despite the elaborate ornamentation used by the builders on most of the houses in Union Park, only two of the houses were faced with brownstone (as opposed to five in Chester Square).

The *1852 Boston Almanac* had noted, "The 108 good house lots in the immediate vicinity of Union Park will soon be covered with genteel private dwellings." The use of the word "genteel" to describe houses that had not yet been built reflected the *Almanac*'s perception of Union Park as a fashionable place to live. As it turned out, although many of the Union Park houses were identical, they all were distinguished by a profusion of ornamental details from pattern books, which would have made them more attractive to prospective middle-class buyers. Although these houses were slightly smaller and less distinguished than those of Chester Square, their average price was

View of Union Park toward Tremont Street, early 1860s. Boston Athenæum.

This view of Union Park looking from Shawmut Avenue toward Tremont Street shows the street trees planted by the city, even though it had recently planted trees within the garden. Beyond the closed gate one fountain is visible, but the white flagpole is not visible against the open sky.

Stereograph of Union Park, early 1860s.
Courtesy of The Bostonian Society/ Old State House.

This view of Union Park shows some of the elaborate ironwork fences enclosing the front yards of the houses on the part of the street just beyond the garden. Also shown are the two arbors placed at the midpoint of the garden, where a five-foot walkway joins them.

around $15,000—about the same as many of the Chester Square brick bowfronts.

Among the individuals who settled in Union Park were several corn merchants and grocers, including the well-known Samuel S. Pierce; manufacturers of shoes and clothing; and Alexander Rice, a paper manufacturer and the mayor of Boston in 1856 and 1857. Union Park's convenient location rather than the style of its dwellings may have been the primary attraction for these residents. In writing to her son, Mrs. Everett remarks, "The Union Park houses are all occupied, and quite stylish tenants they have, too." Mrs. Everett's use of the word "stylish" to describe the residents may reflect her personal impressions rather than her firsthand knowledge of who actually lived there.

Stereographs from around 1860, a time when all the houses had been built, depict the garden's simple original design embellished with contemporary suburban-style flourishes: light-colored arbors that might have contained seating, trellises, a flagpole constructed from a ship's mast, and an assortment of shrubs (possibly rose bushes) in linear flower beds. The pathways appear to have been edged with grass or groundcover borders in a design similar to the one used in Chester Square's garden. Given the relative complexity of the plantings, it was unlikely that the city was able to maintain the garden despite its small size. According to Albert Wolfe, author of the 1906 study *The Lodging-House Problem in Boston*, the property owners in Chester and Worcester squares and Union Park "bore the expense of their maintenance, and had the chief enjoyment of their use." Just as in Chester Square, the residents of Union Park and, later, Worcester Square must have hired a gardener even though the city had promised to take care of the grass and trees. And in Union Park (just like Chester Square) the gates to the garden remained locked, with only the property owners having keys.

Because property sales and construction activity proceeded at a slow rate in both Chester Square and Union Park, it took about ten years before the areas had a full complement of dwellings. In 1855, Mayor J. V. C. Smith had lamented, "A whole year has passed away, leaving very nearly the same quantity of public lands on hand, which the city possessed twelve months ago." It is therefore understandable that in 1857, when the Board of Land Commissioners proposed the creation of another garden square—this one to be called Madison Square—just south of Worcester Square between Harrison Avenue and Albany Street, the Board of Aldermen was not interested. At this time the lots in Worcester Square, the third of the city's new squares, had not yet been auctioned. In championing yet another new square —this time one that would benefit residents of limited means—the land commissioners argued a line of thought that contemporary reformers were advancing. Specifically, public squares in large cities were advantageous in promoting the health and comfort of the inhabitants. The commissioners noted that wealthy families could vacation in the country, whereas poor residents, who also needed "air and exercise," had no other place to go and therefore needed access to outdoor spaces in the immediate vicinity of their homes. Perhaps the commissioners thought that a new square with relatively inexpensive house lots and houses would demonstrate the city's genuine concern about the well-being of its less affluent citizens.

Although the land commissioners had argued for a new garden square based on its health benefits, they must have understood that a garden square with residents of limited means would not be very profitable for the city. They knew that the primary reason for developing a garden square was that the value of the land in the immediate vicinity of the garden would increase substantially. According to the commissioners, this had happened around Union Park (compared to nearby Hanson Street), Chester Square (compared to Concord Street, a few streets away), and Blackstone Square (compared to Canton Street, also a few streets away). There is no doubt that most of the lots in the South End squares had higher values than their counterparts on other streets. The problem was that these higher-priced lots were not selling at the rate the city had expected. Thus, the city had second thoughts about the wisdom of investing even more money in garden infrastructure—especially for a garden square intended for poorer residents.

While lobbying for the creation of Madison Square, the commissioners did attest to the exclusive nature of Chester Square, Union Park, and Worcester Square, which was still without residents. They admitted that these squares were more like private gardens than public squares because they had been "reserved not for the public use so much as for the purpose of beautifying the city and increasing the value of property in their vicinity." Given this acknowledgment, it is not clear how, if they had been successful in getting the city to create another square, the commissioners would have been able to ensure that the lots and houses would have been affordable to the individuals they were trying to attract.

By 1859, with Chester Square and Union Park nearly completed, the city turned its attention to Worcester Square, which had been laid out in 1851 between Harrison Avenue and Washington Street. Perhaps the city's reluctance to develop Worcester Square was the direct result of its relatively unsuccessful auction in Union Park. The decision to postpone an auction that had the potential to generate some revenue was financially risky given the fact that the city had already invested money in preparing the garden. However, the city must have realized within a very short time that relying on garden squares as a tool for keeping Boston's residents from moving to the suburbs might not have been as simple a matter as it had seemed in 1850.

Aaron Allen, a furniture dealer, had built his imposing brownstone mansion at the corner of Washington Street and Worcester Square by 1859. Also, plans were being made for a new Boston City Hospital, designed by Gridley J. F. Bryant in 1861 and completed in 1864, at the opposite end of the square. The notice in the *Boston Daily Evening Transcript* announcing the auction of forty-two lots in Worcester Square, which was to take place on May 10, 1859, stated: "These are among the best lots for the erection of genteel houses of the first class remaining of the public lands and are fully equal to any land now for

sale in that part of the city." It was now very convenient to reach downtown from Worcester Square, for it was located just off Washington Street, which had become a major horsecar route in 1856.

The prospectus for this city land shows a plan of the forty-two lots, with frontages ranging from 24 to 34 feet—with most around 25 feet—and depths from 85 to 105 feet. The city imposed the same building restrictions here as it had on the buyers of lots in Chester Square and Union Park. In addition, however, the Worcester Square prospectus also includes the following stipulation: "A dwelling house, as above described, shall be erected and completed, ready for occupancy, within two years from the first day of May 1859." After almost ten years the city had realized that its building incentives were not effective, and it could no longer afford to allow speculators to take their time in constructing their buildings. This strategy appears to have worked, for by 1861 many of the lots contained houses. Approximately half of the lots sold in 1859; the remainder sold by the end of 1862, when the city noted that nineteen lots on Worcester Square had gone for an average of $.80 per square foot, a figure substantially lower than the $1.00 to $1.27 of three years earlier. This decrease in value presumably reflected the effects of the Civil War.

Compared to their counterparts in Chester Square and Union Park, the houses in Worcester Square were the most uniform in appearance —all brick bowfronts, with mansard roofs and rusticated basements. Other than some minor differences in the styles of their lintels and entrances, the dwellings on each side of the square had consistent designs for their stoop railings—more traditional balustrades on the north side (some punctuated by large, round holes) and scalloped-edged brownstone hand rails on the south side. Although the overall homogeneity of the houses might have indicated that architects were

Worcester Square in a photograph by George H. Drew, mid-1860s. Courtesy of The Bostonian Society/ Old State House.

In this view of Worcester Square, looking toward the newly constructed Boston City Hospital, the uniformity of the row houses, with only the window lintels and balustrades varying from one side to the other, is striking. The gate of the lotus-stalk fence is open, inviting visitors to enter the garden.

not involved in their design, it is known that architect Charles Kirby designed a group of four row houses on the north side. These houses were distinguished by arched entrances that were decorated with carved moldings in the shape of ropes. Because all of the Worcester Square houses were similar in appearance, it is not surprising that they all sold for approximately the same price, about $12,000, which was several thousand dollars less than what their more elaborate counterparts in Chester Square and Union Park had sold for only a few years earlier. The residents of Worcester Square were, in general, relatively unknown merchants and lawyers, who might have been slightly less affluent than the residents of the other squares and who sought the convenience, rather than the prestige, of living in Worcester Square.

The *1852 Boston Almanac* noted that Worcester Square would have the same design as Union Park. Judging from later photos, it is clear that the city had again chosen the lotus-stalk Louisburg Square fence for the perimeter of the garden. At the end of 1851, the city reported expenses for the following improvements: "labor and material in filling Worcester Square (unfinished); and grading, fencing and fitting up fountains." Although the *1852 Almanac* had predicted one fountain instead of the two that soon graced Union Park, the city originally might have installed two fountains in Worcester Square, as was depicted on the 1852 map of Boston. On the other hand, since there were no property owners in 1852, the city may have felt that it could save money by installing just one fountain. An 1862 plan and later photographs of Worcester Square show only one fountain—a traditional Boy-with-a-Dolphin statue that has additional dolphins around the shaft of the upper basin—one similar to a stock pattern in the Janes, Kirtland & Co. catalog in which a fountain like those in Union Park is pictured. The choice of such an elaborate design for only one fountain underscored the city's desire to create a highly ornamental landscape consistent with contemporary Victorian taste. The fact that the 1853 Report of the Superintendent of Public Lands also lists expenses for "grading Worcester Square, setting trees and repairing fence on the same" indicates that the city took care of the garden even when the square had no residents.

Immediately after the auction of house lots in 1859, the city continued its development of Worcester Square. In 1860 it spent money for grading and furnishing loam, as well as $20 for repairing the fence. By 1862, possibly under pressure from the new residents, the city decided to overhaul the garden completely. Resetting the ten-year-old fence must have been the first priority because an 1862 plan of Worcester Square shows the grades of the fence foundation and curbstones. In addition to spending $1,583 to raise the foundation and reset the iron fence—perhaps because it had not been installed properly—

Stereograph of Worcester
Square, mid–1860s.
Private collection.

This view of Worcester Square from above is comparable to the view of
Union Park's garden shown earlier. The original tree pits near the fence
are empty because new trees were planted ten feet closer to the central
path during the resetting of the fence in 1862. The single fountain is
painted white, as was often the custom.

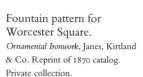

Fountain pattern for
Worcester Square.
Ornamental Ironwork, Janes, Kirtland
& Co. Reprint of 1870 catalog.
Private collection.

The classical motif of a Boy
with a Dolphin, which resembles the statue on Worcester
Square's original fountain, is
shown in an 1870 ironwork
catalog. Although the entire
structure as pictured measures
only five feet two inches tall,
in Worcester Square it was
mounted on a pedestal of rocks
that increased its overall height.

No. 9.

the city also painted the fence, furnished and set curbstones, and
paved the sidewalks. Since all this construction activity must have
destroyed any plantings that existed, the city also furnished "loam,
red gravel, seeds and sods" and purchased and planted new trees.
Although the "red gravel" was most likely intended for the paths, it
could have been used in the planting beds, which were similar in
design to those in Union Park's garden. These additional expenses for
garden improvements meant a smaller return on the city's initial
investment in Worcester Square.

Later Squares

In addition to the five public squares that have been discussed, the
South End had one other narrow garden square, now lost. This
square may have been created around 1851, when it first appeared
on a plot plan. It is not clear who was responsible for creating this
garden square. In any case, contemporary city records did not mention garden-related expenses incurred for the square, as they did for
the other squares. The fact that a narrow, oblong garden was inserted

into a street that as early as 1846 was called Ashland Park—and some-times Ashland Avenue—might have meant that the city had antici-pated the creation of another garden square to attract residents when the street was laid out. The 1848 plan of the South End shows Ash-land Avenue running parallel to and east of Blake's Court between Washington Street and Harrison Avenue in an undeveloped area near Dover Street. The 1851 plan shows a fenced garden measuring 24 feet wide and about 240 feet long, with property owners of narrow lots on one side and one owner—Thayer & Jackson—for all of the property on the other side of the square. A 12-foot-wide area on both sides of the entrance to the square from Washington Street is also fenced in an effort to create an exclusive enclave by creating a buffer zone protecting the residents from those passing by on Wash-ington Street.

In 1855, Mrs. Everett, whose house was located several blocks south on Washington Street, wrote to her son: "Ashland Avenue is now quite a handsome place, with the grass-plot and 3 fountains." The name of the square was changed to Ashland Place in 1853. The sub-stitution of the word "place" for "avenue" connotes an exclusive res-idential enclave and may have been requested by the wealthy resident who moved into a large "brick house" erected on the property for-merly owned by Thayer & Jackson. This detached house, shown on an 1860 plot plan, fronts on Washington Street and has a hundred-foot-deep side garden separating the house from Ashland Place. The owner's interest in further embellishing Ashland Place may have been reflected in the notes written on this plan. The narrow, fenced-in entry areas—"never to be built upon"—and the central garden are: "To be enclosed and laid down to grass and ornamented with trees and shrubbery." The 1860 plan allows room for an eight-foot "pas-sageway" as well as an eight-foot "side-walk" at the entrance from Washington Street but only an eight-foot "passageway & side-walk" around the entire central garden.

By 1874, when the square had bowfront houses on the north side and flat fronts on the south side, the surrounding neighborhood had become a center for the woodworking industry, with several lumber-yards in the vicinity. Ashland Place may have survived as a garden square until shortly before 1896, when it was renamed Laconia Street. The fact that Ashland Place was allowed to disappear, whereas the other South End garden squares remained intact, suggests that its demise was the result of its location in an area that was rapidly becoming the center of light industry. In 1998, with construction of the new Laconia Lofts building in the entire block between Washing-ton Street and Harrison Avenue, the footprint of Laconia Street was lost. Laconia Lofts is a large, mixed-income housing complex with twenty-eight affordable live-work lofts for artists, seventy-one market-rate units, and retail spaces on the ground floor.

In 1859, having finally honored its longstanding commitment to furnish Worcester Square with dwellings and an attractive garden, the city was not in a positive enough financial position to take on the responsibility of creating new garden squares. Experience had confirmed that the market for higher-priced housing in the South End was drying up. However, perhaps as a result of strong interest on the part of new residents, the blocks of Concord and Rutland streets extending west of Tremont Street to Columbus Avenue were soon to become Concord and Rutland squares, respectively, while the block of Pembroke Street west of Columbus Avenue became Berwick Park.

After 1857, as the Boston Water Power Company began filling the area west of Tremont Street, the city took ownership of the newly filled parts of Concord and Rutland streets. This occurred in stages, first, to halfway between Tremont Street and Columbus Avenue, and finally all the way to Columbus Avenue. Around 1860, many new row houses were built on these two blocks starting at the eastern end at Tremont Street. The earliest dwellings in Rutland Square included a unique row of eleven houses in a Venetian-Gothic style on the north side. These dwellings were faced in buff-colored stucco with wooden bays painted with sand to match. Evidence that the city's sale of house lots was influenced by the streets' changing property lines can be seen in the consistent architectural details of the row houses that were constructed in each section, particularly the height of the stoops and style of their railings. The houses in Concord Square were mostly traditional high-stooped brick bowfronts with different styles of balustrades, depending on when they were built.

Starting in 1866, when Concord and Rutland streets were renamed Concord and Rutland squares, the city began to lay out long, narrow gardens in sections that reflected the former Boston Water Power Company property lines. Since this happened several years after many houses had been built and most of the lots had been sold, it is possible that the residents and property owners had requested these gardens. In both squares the house lots were shortened by seven or eight feet, and the public ways were widened in order to accommodate the gardens while still allowing space for carriages. An updated 1866 plan of Rutland Square shows two additional garden sections inserted into the street, which had been newly widened using land taken from abutters. One can only assume that the current and future residents were familiar with Ashland Place's long, narrow garden and wished to have a similar garden both to enhance their streets for their own enjoyment and to increase the value of their property. In all the earlier South End squares, except for Ashland Place, the city had created the gardens as incentives for the sale of house lots, and the auction plans had been drawn accordingly.

Because there was so little extra space in the streets—even when the land taken from the abutters was included—the gardens were less than 20 feet wide, and there was room for only a single row of trees down the middle. The garden in Concord Square was laid out in two sections—one in 1866, the other in 1868. Each section measured approximately 15 feet by 150 feet. A cast-iron fountain might have been placed on a circular island between the two sections at the time that the second section was laid out. The garden in Rutland Square had three sections, each measuring approximately 18 feet by 100 feet. Since the gardens in Concord and Rutland squares were so narrow, it is probable that they originally were not fenced.

As the city laid out the streets on its newly acquired land between Columbus Avenue and the Boston & Providence Railroad tracks, it had one final opportunity to create more narrow garden squares. An 1868 city plan of this property indicates that the city was contemplating narrow garden squares on several of its new streets: Yarmouth and Holyoke streets, West Rutland Square, Greenwich Park, and Pembroke Street (which was renamed Berwick Park in 1869). This plan shows sixteen-foot-wide oblong gardens with house lots at the Columbus Avenue end stepped back in a gentle curve. Eight feet have been taken from the lots along either side of the streets in order to allow for twenty-five-foot-wide carriageways on either side of the gardens. According to the plan, the proposed changes of street lines were "agreed upon by the owners and abutters thereon." With the exception of Berwick Park (renamed Braddock Park in 1918), none of the gardens were ever created—perhaps because neither the abutters nor the city had the money to develop them. An 1870 Plan of Charles Walker's Land on Berwick Park shows six house lots owned by Charles Walker, with lines indicating that eight feet from each lot have been allocated to the city in order to accommodate a narrow garden. Like Concord and Rutland squares, the creation of this final garden square may have been the result of efforts by a builder or the residents rather than the city.

This last burst of energy from the proponents of garden squares was relatively weak compared to that which had produced three new squares in 1850. The gardens of Concord and Rutland squares and Berwick Park were essentially afterthoughts that had been inserted into the streets after many of the house lots had been sold. The row houses in each of these squares sold for prices in the range of $8,000 to $13,000 to individuals who were likely to be employees rather than owners of the new manufacturing companies. Although these small spaces were token gardens—suitable only for viewing—their presence proved, again, that even a small ornamental garden was important to the residents who had chosen to live in the squares.

The story of the planning and execution of the South End squares ends with the creation of an inverted variant of garden squares. Whereas traditional garden squares were always an integral part of the street system, with central gardens bordered by streets and row houses, the South End had three leftover spaces—each in the middle of an entire block of row houses—that ultimately became private, but common, garden spaces. These three gardens—Leighton Park, now lost, and Carlton and Montgomery parks, both of which still exist—were not only owned by the abutters but also were accessible only to the residents whose houses backed onto the gardens.

Leighton Park was located in the middle of the block bounded by Dartmouth and Yarmouth streets, Columbus Avenue, and Truro Street, which no longer exists. It appears unnamed in the 1874 city atlas, and is named in the 1888 atlas.

Carlton Park is a 3,132-square-foot-space that was reserved for use as a park as early as 1870. Located in the middle of the block bounded by Columbus and Warren avenues and West Canton Street, it currently is owned by some but not all the abutters. Carlton Park was greatly reduced in size when the owners of a large apartment house at the corner of Columbus and Warren avenues covered a sizeable section of the garden space with concrete and installed permanent concrete benches. The remaining small garden—which includes a large linden tree in the center surrounded by grass, a few flowers, ferns, and overgrown shrubs—now resembles someone's backyard rather than a large communal garden. The individual backyards of the houses are fenced, with the result that they are completely private and do not serve as visual extensions of the main garden.

Montgomery Park, located in the center of the block bounded by Montgomery, Dartmouth, West Canton, and Tremont streets, is a trapezoidal space that originally was only slightly larger than Carlton Park. It was first shown—and named—on a "Plan of Estates belonging to E. Baker, Esq., to be sold at public auction on February 7, 1865." An early photo shows a wooden fence surrounding the garden. Montgomery Park is now an attractive grassy lawn with trees, flowerbeds, and a narrow brick path running between the perimeter of the common garden and the small private yards that back onto the garden but are not divided from it by tall fences, as they are in Carlton Park.

These interior gardens were their developers' solution to laying out house lots on property that was not rectangular because the bordering thoroughfares of Columbus Avenue and Dartmouth Street were located at an angle to the South End grid. The developers must have thought that the most effective use of these three irregularly shaped blocks was to place row houses along the perimeter streets and create a garden in back with the leftover space. Instead of providing all the residents with a service alley that bisected the block—as the city had done in almost every block of the South End, including those that fronted on squares—each developer offered the amenity of a private interior garden, which he hoped would attract potential buyers.

It is interesting that London, too, has many examples of what could be termed "inverted" squares, such as the mid-nineteenth-century Ladbroke Square, where access to the gardens was limited to the residents whose private back gardens abutted a large communal garden. In both London and the South End, living in a garden square, where everyone could see the garden for which a premium had been paid, was still more prestigious than living in a house that backed onto a common garden.

Although Bulfinch introduced the garden square to Boston, his Franklin Place was conceived as a single real estate venture. Likewise, the developers of Louisburg and Pemberton squares were only interested in creating a single garden square. Although these squares were small, their successful development was very labor-intensive. Not only did the lots have to be sold and the houses built, but the garden had to be completed and maintained. Beginning with Bulfinch's Columbia Square in 1801, the city had planned Boston's South End as a separate and cohesive district enhanced by a group of eight garden squares (not including Ashland Place) that were planned over a period of seventy years. Yet Boston was not unique in discovering that garden squares could easily be replicated within a small geographical area, for London had already begun to use this form of planning. Only a large property owner, such as the city of Boston or the London estate landlord, had the financial resources to take on the task of developing a series of squares.

London's Bloomsbury Estate

In many ways Boston's use of garden squares that could be created on an as-needed basis was the same as the process undertaken in developing London's Bloomsbury Estate. Bloomsbury, which occupied an area about half the size of the South End at mid-century, was located about one mile from London's business center and ultimately contained seven squares created over an almost two-hundred-year period. There were only two significant differences between the London and Boston real estate ventures. In Boston, a public agency assumed the role of developer. The city sold lots to speculators, who, in turn, built houses that they sold to residents. In London, the developer was a private estate owner, who maintained control of the houses through ninety-nine-year leases.

A comparison of the South End to the Bloomsbury Estate shows that both developers took advantage of the fact that garden squares were relatively small urban landscape forms that were especially suited to replication in a variety of shapes and sizes within a small geographical area. The gardens in Bloomsbury's squares ranged in size from Russell Square, the largest, with an area of more than ten acres, and Bedford Square, with approximately five acres, to the smallest gardens—Torrington and Woburn squares—which were similar in shape to several of the South End squares. Each of the other three gardens—Bloomsbury, Tavistock, and Gordon—was somewhat less than five acres in size. The gardens varied in shape, with Bedford being oval like the South End's early Columbia Square (which was later squared off); Bloomsbury, Tavistock, and Gordon being rectangular; and Torrington and Woburn being oblong with rounded ends. As in the South End, the Bloomsbury squares were not laid out in any discernible pattern except for Russell Square, which was connected to Bloomsbury Square by Bedford Place, a street one block long.

In many but not all respects, the city and the estate owner had the same goals and therefore assumed similar roles in planning their respective districts. The immediate economic goal of both the estate owner and the city of Boston was to make their developments as enticing as possible to both speculative builders and prospective residents by creating squares with beautiful gardens. Because the estate owner could afford to ignore immediate profits in favor of enhancing the long-term value of his estate, he was willing to make loans to builders as inducements for erecting higher-quality dwellings. The city of Boston, on the other hand, eventually provided financial incentives to speculators to build houses as quickly as possible rather than to build better houses. Despite this difference, both the city and the estate owner had total control over the planning and layout of streets in the squares and their attendant infrastructure—paving, drainage, and sewers—as well as the overall design (height and material restrictions) and function (residential use) of all buildings on the property.

On the Bloomsbury Estate the squares were laid out one at a time, as the landowner perceived a demand for housing. In 1665, in his first attempt to make this sort of profit from his property, the Earl of Southampton laid out Bloomsbury Square in front of his own mansion. It was not until 110 years later, in 1775, that the then-current earl perceived a new market, housing for an affluent middle class, and created the well-known Bedford Square. Russell Square was developed in 1800, just before the building boom ended. Work on Tavistock Square did not begin until 1821, after which two smaller squares —Torrington and Woburn—were inserted into the existing street plan. The building depression of the 1830s brought new construction to a virtual halt in Bloomsbury. Finally, Gordon Square was laid out in the 1840s but was not completed until 1860.

By developing one square at a time, the landowner was not burdened with too many empty house lots or unleased houses. The city of Boston, in contrast, planned several squares simultaneously and even completed the gardens, but it did not try to sell off lots until there was a perceived demand for more housing. The problem with the Boston approach was that without residents serving as watchdogs, the garden could languish—as it had done in Worcester Square.

Bloomsbury's terrace houses were very similar in style to the South End's row houses, largely because both London and Boston had codified building restrictions for attached houses. Generally not all the houses in any one square in either Bloomsbury or the South End were identical (because they were usually built by different speculators at different times), yet the dwellings tended to be quite uniform. Mews (that is, stables) were built in back of some of the Bloomsbury squares, including Bedford and Russell, as a convenience for the residents. In the South End, although most of the houses backed onto service alleys, wooden stables were often grouped together on nearby streets.

An important element of the Bloomsbury Estate's long-range plan was attracting respectable leaseholders. The landowner did not wish to improve the circumstances of the residents but, rather, to provide a particular class of people—middle-class people—with the comforts and amenities to which they were already accustomed. Although Bedford Square at its height was probably the best address in Bloomsbury, it was not an aristocratic enclave like other garden squares in central London. In this respect the South End, with its prospering middle-class residents, was quite similar to Bloomsbury. In the end, both the South End and Bloomsbury were successful in attracting fairly affluent middle-class residents.

Because the gardens in both the Bloomsbury and the South End squares were planned as centerpieces that would attract affluent buyers, it is important to compare the roles played by the private and public developers in creating and maintaining these gardens. As owners of their respective gardens, both the estate and the city assumed most of the responsibilities and costs of completing the gardens, with the estate owner reimbursing the builders for performing the actual work of forming and enclosing the gardens. However, the responsibility for maintaining the gardens differed from Bloomsbury to the South End. The estate tended to rely more heavily on contributions from its leaseholders. The leases usually contained covenants according to which the lessees would pay a share of the annual cost of maintaining the gardens. When major repairs were necessary—for instance, rebuilding the fences, adding new gravel to the walks, or re-landscaping the garden—the estate provided financial assistance. In the South End, where the city had initially committed to completing and maintaining the gardens, it could not require residents to pay for services that the public sector had promised to provide. In some cases the residents in the squares, not satisfied with the quality of these services, decided to hire their own gardeners.

This comparison of the South End to Bloomsbury makes it clear that creating and managing a multiplicity of garden squares for financial profit, whether in Bloomsbury or the South End, required similar strategies. However, the city, burdened by debt and many competing needs, could offer only minimal financial incentives to builders. The estate owner, being in a financial position that permitted taking a longer-term view, was able to subsidize the work of builders in order to produce higher-quality houses. Despite the relative wealth of the estate owner, the financial success of his squares was still subject to the vagaries of London's economy, just as the success of the South End squares depended on the condition of Boston's economy from year to year.

Chapter Three

EVOLUTION AND PRESERVATION

*T*HE SOUTH END SQUARES were flourishing and fashionable residential enclaves for a relatively short time. Despite the squares' ornate dwellings and lovely gardens, the affluent middle-class residents, for whom the city had created and embellished the squares starting in 1850, began to move out in the early 1870s. Franklin Place and Pemberton Square managed to retain their exclusive status for almost fifty years, even with the increasing encroachment of commercial interests. Yet the loss of some of the wealthiest citizens from the South End squares was an early warning of the impending decline of the entire district.

Because it was highly unusual for such an attractive and prestigious neighborhood to fall out of favor so quickly, the South End became the subject of some of the earliest sociological studies of urban problems as well as the setting for a novel, *The Rise of Silas Lapham*, written in 1884. Its author, William Dean Howells (1837–1920), lived in Louisburg Square during the 1870s when he was editor of *The Atlantic Monthly*. His novel provides a contemporary view of a period when the South End's garden squares rapidly lost their prestige. The book's hero, Silas Lapham, was a paint manufacturer who bought a house on the fictional oval-shaped Nankeen Square in 1863 from "a terrified gentleman of good extraction who discovered too late that the South End was not the thing." By 1875, Silas, wishing to move his family to a more fashionable neighborhood, decided to build a fancy "brownstone front" with a "French roof" on property he had previously purchased on the "water side" of Beacon Street in the Back Bay—or "New Land," as he called it. In real life, South End resident Aaron Allen, the furniture magnate who in 1859 had built the impressive brownstone mansion still standing at the Washington Street end of Worcester Square, in similar fashion left for the "water side" of Beacon Street in the Back Bay in 1871.

Since the South End's eight garden squares were miniature neighborhoods within a larger district, it is not surprising that their evolution mirrored the history of the South End from the beginning of its downward spiral in the early 1870s to the start of rehabilitation efforts in the district a century later. The fact that the South End became a low-income community with little new construction for a hundred years meant that most of the garden squares—both houses and gardens—remained intact during this period. Although most of the single-family row houses were converted into lodging houses and the gardens were neglected and became overgrown, these garden squares, forgotten and frozen in time, were to be discovered and reclaimed along with the rest of the South End a century later. In the 1970s, a wave of middle- and upper-middle-class owners brought to the squares a new emphasis on private stewardship and preservation. As an example of history repeating itself, this phenomenon occurred more than a hundred years after the city had made a major financial investment to create squares that invited and encouraged the very same type of homeowner to move to the new South End.

Decline of the South End

It is doubtful that either the city or the state could have predicted that the Back Bay would so quickly eclipse the South End as the most fashionable new place to live. Developed by the state in 1857 on filled land between what is now Arlington Street to the east, Massachusetts Avenue to the west, Beacon Street to the north, and Boylston Street to the south, the Back Bay held many attractions. Its proximity to the Charles River, the Public Garden, and Beacon Hill was appealing, as were the presence of a French-style boulevard named Commonwealth Avenue and the elegant French-style brownstone row houses, a welcome change from the South End's old-fashioned brick bowfronts. For established Beacon Hill families, the Back Bay had the additional benefit of allowing the younger generation to remain close to the rest of the family. Still it would be surprising if a group of South End residents uprooted themselves after only ten or fifteen years simply to participate in the latest residential fashion parade. Although fickle fashion may have been partly responsible for the flight of some of the South End's most affluent residents to the Back Bay, economic and social forces also were at work in the South End, prompting an exodus to other areas of the city.

In creating the South End squares at mid-century, the city was able to take advantage of a burgeoning economy. Although Boston was eclipsed by New York as the nation's center of finance and commerce during the 1830s and 1840s, Boston's transition from a mercantile city to a manufacturing city was, on the whole, very successful and promising. At mid-century the city's middle and upper classes exhibited great confidence in both their business ventures and their social activities. Unfortunately this optimism was to be shattered less than a quarter of a century later, when Boston's Great Fire of 1872 destroyed a huge area downtown, a total of sixty-five acres of retail and wholesale establishments. Although this area was rebuilt within a short time, the city promptly suffered the effects of the country's Great Panic of 1873. Nationally, the Panic resulted in thousands of business failures and a massive increase in unemployment; and in the South End, banks foreclosed on speculative buildings, which had been the mainstay of the district's real estate development. Even though the country's economy had recovered by 1880, the South End's future remained blighted, at least for the next century.

Despite the relative success of the city's initial efforts to stem the tide of departing middle-class residents through the creation of garden squares, by the 1870s it was clear that these efforts had outlived their usefulness. As Boston's population doubled between 1850 and 1870 and then doubled again by 1900, when it reached about five hundred thousand, neighborhoods close to the downtown area became overcrowded and began to deteriorate. Those who had the means to do so moved to the newly developing suburbs in pursuit of freestanding wood-frame houses with ample yards. This exodus was facilitated first by the improved and expanded street railway lines introduced in 1852, and then by the electric cars introduced in 1889. Between 1870 and 1900, except for the dwellings in the Back Bay and workers' tenements downtown and in the South End, most new housing was built in the suburbs.

As many middle- and upper-middle-class residents moved to the suburbs or the Back Bay, the fancy houses that they vacated in the squares no longer were the symbols of respectability on which their original owners had once lavished money and attention. By 1900 most of these single-family dwellings had been converted into lodging houses, which functioned as residences for the South End's growing population of clerks, salespeople, skilled mechanics, and industrial workers, many of whom were immigrants. The Boston Elevated Railway, completed in 1901 and not dismantled until 1987, ran along Washington Street from downtown through the South End. With this unattractive intrusion, the formerly prestigious locations of Blackstone, Franklin, and Worcester squares—all abutting Washington Street and consequently subjected to the constant onslaught of soot, noise, and darkness—continued to decline.

Lodging houses, in contrast to apartment houses and tenements, usually consisted of separate rooms rented to single men and women or to couples without children, who took their meals elsewhere. According to Albert Wolfe, author of the 1906 work *The Lodging-House Problem in Boston*, by the turn of the century five-sixths of the South End's row houses had become lodging houses, making the South End the country's largest rooming-house district. Wolfe's study, which tracked the number of real-estate transfers on Union Park between 1868 and 1902, determined that the greatest number of the square's residents decided to sell their houses between 1885 and 1890, largely because of declining real estate values. This period coincided with the time when the city as a whole experienced its slowest rate of growth and the suburbs the fastest. Although the exodus from the squares by those most influenced by fashion had begun much earlier, it took a while for the majority of residents to be convinced that, since the neighborhood had begun to deteriorate, they too should sell their houses.

Only the "Rooms to Let" signs affixed to the exteriors of the formerly stylish row houses that had been built forty years earlier revealed the dwellings' recent transformation into lodging houses. The internal layout of the typical row house, with two large rooms and one small side room per floor, lent itself to a functional lodging-house configuration that could accommodate as many lodgers as there were rooms. The major problem with the row houses was that most of them contained only one full bathroom plus a servants' bathroom in the basement, and this arrangement was rarely able to service a large number of lodgers. The new tenements and apartment houses that were built in the South End at this time were divided into suites of rooms, each with its own housekeeping facilities and a bathroom that could accommodate families.

Because the population of the South End was now composed almost exclusively of workers who left their lodging houses early in the morning and did not return until evening, the entire district remained a deserted no-man's land during the day. In the squares, where there had once been the constant bustle of affluent middle-class life—"liveried coachmen and white-capped nursemaids airing their charges," according to Wolfe—there now were only worn façades of buildings that had seen better days and neglected gardens that once had been carefully tended. The garden squares that the city had created to attract successful middle-class residents had not been able to compete with either the Back Bay's prestigious location and stylish architecture or the larger house lots that the suburbs could offer.

In 1892, the South End House, Boston's first settlement and the precursor to the United South End Settlements, was created as a gathering place where people could discuss social problems and advocate for neighborhood improvements. In 1901, the South End House was relocated from Rollins Street to 20 Union Park, where it served as the headquarters of the United South End Settlements until 1975. The South End House demonstrated its value as a sociological laboratory by publishing several comprehensive studies written by its residents. *The Lodging-House Problem in Boston*, referred to earlier, *The City Wilderness*, written in 1898 by social worker Robert Woods (1865–1925), and *Neighbors All*, the personal recollections of social worker Esther G. Barrows, provide an excellent overview of life in the South End at the turn of the century. Focusing primarily on economic and social activities, these books contain only passing references to the gardens in the South End squares. But even at the turn of the century, the squares seemed to be relatively pleasant enclaves compared to the dingy and overcrowded housing that existed nearby. Wolfe noted that "some of the prettiest places in Boston today" were the "squares" of the South End lodging-house district, such as "West Chester Park," Worcester Square, and Union Park. Woods described the squares as "still outwardly as pleasant places of abode as can be found within the main city."

In 1899, *The Ladies Home Journal* published a series of articles by Anna Farquhar, a recent visitor to Boston, that were subsequently collected in a book, *Her Boston Experiences*. Even though these first impressions of Boston deal primarily with its well-known cultural attractions—the museum, the new library, Trinity Church, and the Symphony—at the turn of the century, the author must have been familiar with the South End, which she describes as "like a young man who, starting out in life with brilliant prospects and making an utter failure of himself, gradually and reluctantly falls below the point of respectability." Anna Farquhar appears to have visited Columbus Avenue as well as Braddock Park (still called Berwick Park) and also probably Concord and Rutland squares. She describes this neighborhood as follows:

> Running off of this avenue are the most interesting domestic squares in Boston. The homes date from the beginning of the South End, and are mostly of English urban architecture with low stoops. These houses are built of brick enriched in color by time, and during six months of the year embowered in ivy. A refreshing plot of green grass and trees runs between the curved line of houses, and all is quiet, restful, and dignified.

This description, which matches closely photographs of these three squares taken around 1910, confirms that at the turn of the century these garden squares were still attractive enclaves.

During the decline of the South End, there was almost no photographic documentation of either the houses or the gardens in the

Chester Square looking
west, ca. 1896.
Courtesy of The South End
Historical Society.

At the end of the nineteenth century, Chester Square, unlike Blackstone and Franklin squares, still has its original lotus-stalk fence; and the
fountain, flagpole, and tool shed are also intact. However, since the
snow only seems to be several inches deep, it is obvious that few shrubs
remain, and there are no benches.

squares. Since the buildings, constructed of brick, were relatively durable, the exteriors of the houses remained largely unchanged despite years of neglect. The landscapes were much more ephemeral. Fortunately blueprints—commissioned by the city in 1913—exist for these gardens. Inasmuch as the plans indicate the presence or absence of important features (such as fencing, fountains, and trees) sixty years after the city's initial capital investment, they serve as an important benchmark for tracing the evolution of the gardens.

The 1913 Surveys

By 1911, possibly in response to the park reform movement that was gathering momentum in Boston, the superintendent of the Public Grounds Department and staff members in the mayor's office realized that Boston's many squares and small parks were in urgent need of general improvements. Since the superintendent knew that his own annual appropriation could not cover these improvements, he singled out only the forty-three squares and parks that would qualify for funding through the George F. Parkman bequest. The 1887 will of Mr. Parkman, a wealthy Boston attorney who lived on Beacon Street across from Boston Common, stated that "income is to be used for the improvement of the Common and other parks now existing." Since all the South End squares had been created before 1887, they were eligible for funding.

The repairs that the superintendent recommended for the gardens in the South End squares indicated that the city had probably not paid much attention to these gardens since their creation in the mid-1800s. During the years that the South End was a fashionable neighborhood, the abutters of the gardens had assumed most of the responsibility for their care. Now that the district as a whole had deteriorated, the city must have felt an obligation to upgrade these public spaces so that they might better serve as amenities for the community. Even though the grass and trees in the gardens had been neglected after their former stewards left, most of the recommendations addressed traditional park furnishings rather than plantings. The only recommendations related to vegetation were for "loam and manure" in Franklin Square at an estimated cost of three hundred dollars and "replanting" in Union Park estimated at two hundred dollars. Perhaps the city felt that plantings were more difficult and costly to maintain and less important than traditional park furniture.

Several improvements suggested for the three largest squares— Blackstone, Franklin, and Chester—represented amenities that were typical of the early twentieth century, when park reformers focused

Blackstone Square, ca. 1910.
Boston Picture File, Fine Arts
Department, Boston Public Library;
Reproduced with the permission of
the Trustees of the Public Library.

Looking across Blackstone
Square toward the corner of
West Newton Street and Shawmut Avenue, this photograph
shows men reading newspapers,
most likely after a day of work.
This photo was taken shortly
before the city recommended
that the benches on which the
men are sitting be replaced with
"permanent concrete settees."

on offering facilities that would serve a range of users. An "apparatus
for an up-to-date sand garden" was recommended for Blackstone
Square, and "comfort stations" were recommended for both Franklin
and Chester squares. Other improvements proposed by the superintendent included new iron fences for Worcester Square and the three
smallest squares (Concord and Rutland squares and Berwick Park,
which was renamed Braddock Park in 1918), permanent "concrete
settees" for the five oldest squares, and drinking fountains for all the
squares.

In 1913, before implementing the superintendent's recommendations, the city hired the Olmsted Brothers firm to draw up topographical plans of the city's forty-three small squares and parks, showing elevations in addition to all existing features, including fences,
walks, fountains, and trees. If there were any benches in Blackstone,
Franklin, or Chester squares at the time, they were not shown. By
examining these plans for the gardens of seven of the South End's
squares (the plan of Berwick Park seems to have been lost), one can
imagine what they looked like sixty years after their creation. The

plans are especially enlightening regarding the original configuration of the walks and trees in the seven gardens.

On the 1913 plans of Blackstone and Franklin squares, except for the addition of an extra path or "desire line" traversing the grass, the layout of gravel walks leading to a central fountain is identical to the configuration shown on the 1852 map of Boston. These 1913 plans do not indicate any fences. The original fences must have disappeared sometime before 1900, since photographs from the early twentieth century show short stakes around the perimeter of the two gardens. Because of the large size of these gardens, the superintendent, operating under budgetary constraints, had chosen not to recommend new fences for these two squares in 1911.

The most striking feature of the 1913 plans for Blackstone and Franklin squares is the large number of elms planted by the city in the late 1840s when it was upgrading the gardens with new fences and fountains. The 1913 plans not only show that twenty-six elms had been planted twenty feet apart along the perimeter of each quadrant within the garden but also that a large number of elms had been

Concord Square, ca. 1910. Boston Picture File, Fine Arts Department, Boston Public Library; Reproduced with the permission of the Trustees of the Public Library.

This view of Concord Square, looking from Tremont Street to Columbus Avenue, shows two urns on stone pedestals in one garden section and a cast-iron fountain surrounded by a circular iron fence between the two sections. It is not surprising that the city would soon recommend the installation of a new iron fence around the gardens.

planted about thirty feet apart along the edges of the brick walks surrounding each garden. In 1913, many of these original trees, now with an average diameter of two feet, were still standing.

The 1913 Olmsted Brothers plans of Chester Square and its Chester Park mall (renamed Massachusetts Avenue in 1894) show the same form and dimensions as the 1850 plan and the identical configuration of curvilinear paths as the 1852 map of Boston. The fence surrounding the garden is not of the original Louisburg Square–style lotus pattern but rather is like the one that is still standing in Union Park. The similarity between them suggests that sometime between 1896 (when a photograph of Chester Square shows the original fence) and 1913 the city had replaced the original fences in both squares. The fountain in Chester Square is still in place, and a flagpole stands at the end of the straight path on the north side of the fountain. The plan shows three granite bases located twenty-three feet from either side of the long walkways. A small tool house is situated where the fourth granite base might have been. The granite bases might have supported cast-iron urns holding flowers. The drinking fountain indicated near

Rutland Square, ca. 1910. Boston Picture File, Fine Arts Department, Boston Public Library; Reproduced with the permission of the Trustees of the Public Library.

As shown in this photograph, the first section of Rutland Square, which is closest to Tremont Street, is similar to the garden in Concord Square. Rutland Square has five elm trees in each of its three sections. In 1911 the city had also targeted this square for a new fence. Without automobiles, the narrow square seems quite spacious.

the west entrance of the garden apparently required refurbishing, for the superintendent had suggested that Chester Square needed a new one.

Because so few trees remain within Chester Square's garden, it is difficult to discern the configuration in which they originally had been planted. Elms along the paths seem to have been planted randomly, whereas elms near the ends of the paths in the area surrounding the fifty-foot-wide fountain basin might have been planted in a circular pattern. Of the seven elms shown around the fountain, two must have been original to the garden, for they are more than three feet in diameter. Trees (they were not identified as elms) are spaced approximately twenty-five feet apart on the street edge of the sidewalks. A single row of elm trees extends the entire length of the Chester Park mall from Columbus Avenue to Albany Street. At some point this row had replaced the original double row of elms. The fence originally running along both sides of the mall no longer exists. Just as with Blackstone and Franklin squares, the city's 1911 recommendations for Chester Square had focused on reconstructing the

Berwick Park, ca. 1910. Boston Picture File, Fine Arts Department, Boston Public Library; Reproduced with the permission of the Trustees of the Public Library.

In this view of Berwick Park, looking from Columbus Avenue to the railroad tracks, it is not clear if the garden, which is embellished with urns on stone pedestals, is divided into two sections. Even though the city soon recommended a new fence for this square, for some reason it was never installed.

walks and adding a comfort station rather than on upgrading the plantings, which had appeared to be lush in mid-nineteenth-century photographs.

After 1901, Worcester Square would have been subjected to the dirt and noise generated by the elevated railway passing overhead on Washington Street, so it is not surprising that the 1913 plans of Union Park and Worcester Square show these two squares of identical size in different states of disrepair. In 1903, the city had installed a replacement fence in Union Park that was identical to the one it had installed in Chester Square. Although photographs of Worcester Square taken in the 1880s show the original fence, city records indicate that the fence was removed in 1888. The 1913 plan of Worcester Square shows the square without a fence even though the superintendent had recommended one in 1911. In 1913, Union Park still had two fountains set into basins, each fifteen feet in diameter, whereas in Worcester Square there was no indication of an existing fountain. The flagpole depicted at the center of Union Park had appeared in early photographs of that square.

Although the condition of Union Park in comparison to Worcester Square seemed to reflect more attention by the city, the trees in Worcester Square had fared much better than those in Union Park. Of Union Park's original twenty-four elm trees spaced twenty to twenty-five feet apart (approximately seventeen feet from the central path and very close to the fence), only thirteen remained in 1913, of which seven measured more than two feet in diameter. In Worcester Square, however, twenty elm trees remained, of which eleven measured more than two feet in diameter. In 1862, when these trees were planted after the fence had been reset, they were placed much closer to the central path. Perhaps some of the trees in Union Park suffered major root damage when the new fence was installed in the early twentieth century.

Fortunately three photographs exist that reveal the appearance of the narrow gardens of the South End's three newest squares—Concord and Rutland squares and Berwick Park—at the turn of the century. These photographs show oblong grass plats with urns containing flowers. A fountain appears between the two garden sections of Concord Square. The fences that enclose the gardens are makeshift and not very attractive. Despite their extremely narrow configuration, the city considered these gardens important enough to be surveyed in 1913. The plan of Berwick Park appears lost, but from the plans of Concord and Rutland squares it is possible to ascertain the original placement of the trees in each garden. In 1913, there were six elm trees in the western section of Concord Square and seven in the eastern section. Rutland Square had five elms in each of its three sections.

The new iron fences that the superintendent recommended for Concord and Rutland squares in 1911 were the only improvements that can actually be documented as having been made to the South End squares after the Olmsted Brothers' surveys. In September of 1913 the city drew up plans for a new "iron picket fence" for Concord and Rutland squares that was identical to the fences then existing in Chester Square and Union Park. (If the city did have a survey of Berwick Park, it is interesting that this square was not slated for a new fence.) In both squares, a gate was also to be provided in the fence for each section, and the curb and existing fence around the fountain in Concord Square (which was of the same design as the proposed fences) were also to be repaired. Funds for these fences most likely came from the Parkman Fund.

Although there are no written records indicating that any of the superintendent's other recommendations were implemented, photographs of Franklin and Worcester squares from the 1920s and 1930s and a painting of Chester Square done in 1947 show permanent concrete and wood benches of the type recommended for the five oldest

Fountain in Franklin Square in a photograph by Leslie Jones. 1928.
Courtesy of the Boston Public Library, Print Department.

This view of Franklin Square shows a group of children enjoying the fountain on a hot day. The concrete and wood benches recommended by the city in 1911 are visible lining the paths around the fountain. In the background is the elevated railway running along Washington Street.

Worcester Square in a photograph by Leslie Jones, ca. 1930.
Courtesy of the Boston Public Library, Print Department.

Although in 1911 the city had recommended a new fence for Worcester Square, this photograph indicates that the fence was never installed, but concrete and wood benches were placed in the garden. Many of the original elm trees are still standing.

squares. It is probable that the ten-thousand-dollar expenditure of Parkman funds spent in 1913 for projects in small parks and squares was also used to cover the cost of new benches for the five larger squares as well as the cost of new fences for Concord and Rutland squares.

In 1921, the city decided that it would no longer use money from Parkman's trust fund in any of the squares, even though its own resources for maintaining parks were limited. The 1921 report on expenditures of the Parkman Fund concludes that in restricting his bequest to "parks now existing," Mr. Parkman had not intended that his money be used for the improvement of squares. The report notes that Mr. Parkman would have been familiar with the "country landscapes" that Frederick Law Olmsted, Sr., was creating in Boston during the 1880s. The city's squares, although older than Olmsted's parks, were too small to be able to provide the type of rural ambiance that he had advocated. Unfortunately, once the city eliminated squares from the list of pre-1887 parks covered by the Parkman Fund, it seemed to lose all interest in caring for them.

Robert Woods, author of the previously mentioned *City Wilderness*, was a local social worker who described the South End in 1898 as a wilderness, "with all the dangers to moral and material well being." He anticipated that the area would continue to be a funnel for immigrant groups, with Russian and Polish Jews, Italians, Syrians, and Greeks supplanting the Irish, who were moving to Roxbury and Dorchester in pursuit of more spacious living quarters. Woods also correctly predicted that the lodging houses would deteriorate and be replaced by tenements as an increasing number of small manufacturing establishments began to encroach on former residential streets. Founder of the South End House, Woods was confident that settlement houses could provide moral and physical guidance to the hundreds of poor and unskilled workers who lived in the South End.

Esther Barrows's depiction of the South End during the years after World War I confirms Woods's prediction that the Irish would soon move to what Woods termed "zones of emergence" just beyond the heart of the city. According to Barrows, "This move indicates the ability to pay not only higher rent, but also car fares for such members of the family as work; for the South End is the limit of walking distance from most of the jobs in the city proper." Barrows notes that Syrians, Armenians, and Jews felt much more comfortable acquiring inexpensive real estate in the South End than did the Irish, who chose to invest in two- or three-family houses in the outlying districts.

Barrows offers some interesting insights into the South End residents' outdoor recreational needs during this post-war period. At one point during the summer heat a group of female immigrants appealed to the managers of the elevated railroad to run a special car each day to take residents to and from the Olmsted-designed Franklin Park in West Roxbury. Barrows acknowledges the power of women in influencing those in City Hall: "We did not have the vote, but we had the appeal of the need of little children, which was, and always will be, a great weapon." She notes that women residents had succeeded in getting a small playground built for little children in Franklin Square. According to Barrows, this playground, which was still in existence in the late 1920s, attracted five hundred children a day during the summer. The drinking fountains that the city had installed along some sidewalks (and in 1911 had recommended for placement in the squares) offered welcome relief to many residents.

The few existing photos of the South End squares during the 1920s and 1930s show the gardens with concrete and wooden benches that were emblematic of traditional park furniture of the period. The image of the squares as exclusive residential enclaves was a distant

Union Park looking toward
Shawmut Avenue in a
photograph by Nishan
Bichajian, 1954.
Nishan Bichajian, Courtesy of
Kepes/Lynch Collection. Rotch
Visual Collections, M.I.T.

At this time, Union Park is the
South End square that reflects
the most care by its residents.
Although shrubs have been
planted in a random arrangement, several of the original
elm trees remain, planted close
to the fence. The fence that is
shown replaced the original one
in 1903.

memory. A picture of Chester Square, painted in 1947 by Thomas
Fransioli, Jr. (American 1906–1996), shows a rather desolate-looking
garden with a few large trees, the original three-tiered fountain, the
tool house, and several concrete and wood benches. Since the artist is
known to have painted other, more popular Boston scenes—Louisburg Square, Beacon Hill, and Copley Square—he must have been
impressed with Chester Square, which, although it had seen better
days, still retained traces of its former glory.

In the 1920s and 1930s, many Syrian and Lebanese families had
flocked to Union Park, where several of them operated lodging
houses. Since lodging houses did not provide meals, by this time more
than a hundred inexpensive basement cafeterias and coffee houses had
opened to feed the South End residents. After the Depression and
World War II, saloons, liquor stores, and poolrooms began to eclipse
these small restaurants. By 1945, many stable, working-class immigrant families began to move out, to be replaced by returning veter-
ans and other unemployed people. By the early 1950s, the South End
had become notorious as a skid row or slum area that the city had
chosen to ignore.

The destruction of the garden in Chester Square, located at the edge of the South End bordering on the Roxbury section of Boston, occurred in 1952—just about one hundred years after the city had created it. The original garden was slashed in half to make room for six lanes of commuter traffic coming into the city from the newly constructed Southeast Expressway. What had once been the South End's most elegant garden was reduced to two narrow gardens, each the size of Union Park's garden. The twenty-foot mall extending from both ends of the garden was reduced to a ten-foot median strip.

Having already turned its back on the South End, the city must have considered Chester Square's garden (situated in the middle of Massachusetts Avenue, a potentially major thoroughfare leading from the expressway) completely expendable. The lodgers who resided in Chester Square were too poor to take a proprietary interest in the garden, in contrast to the original mid-nineteenth-century residents, who had devoted so much time to enhancing the garden. Unlike the early-nineteenth-century property owners in Blackstone and Franklin squares—who, having paid a premium for their properties, had reason to contest the city's decision to cut a hundred feet off each garden—the residents of Chester Square were powerless to influence the city.

The 1952 plan showing the proposed relocation of Massachusetts Avenue through Chester Square depicts a garden that bears little resemblance to the original garden. The former curvilinear stone-dust paths have been eliminated, and only the straight paths paved in asphalt remain. The iron fence shown on the 1913 plan still encloses the garden, but on the plan there is an indication that at some time after 1913 approximately fifteen feet have been shaved off the ends of the garden to make the carriageways wider at the curved ends. By 1952, what had formerly been a lush garden with many trees and shrubs had been transformed into a neglected garden with seven elms and two maples. All the street trees outside the garden were gone. Although several benches lined the central path, many others seemed to have been scattered in a random pattern that might have reflected the earlier curvilinear paths. The fountain still occupied the center of the garden, although no doubt it had long before ceased operating. The flagpole and drinking fountain, both of which were shown on the 1913 plan, were still there.

In 1952, the city's Parks Department prepared a landscape plan for the two remaining narrow gardens on either side of Massachusetts Avenue. Each garden was to have fifteen Norway maples, a variety of flowering shrubs, curvilinear flower beds, and seven park benches placed in a row directly across from the houses and in front of a new chain-link fence. It is probable that this landscape plan was implemented because several large maple trees currently remain in the gardens. Although the square's houses were still basically intact, they no longer formed an architectural enclosure around one central garden. Massachusetts Avenue was a devastating intrusion that destroyed the historic integrity of Chester Square.

Urban Renewal and Renaissance

In 1963, the South End was selected as a blighted urban neighborhood to be demolished and rebuilt using federal funding, which focused attention on this derelict area that had been languishing for almost a century. Two nearby urban renewal projects completed in the 1950s had already demonstrated the city's insensitivity to the needs of its current residents. The area just northeast of the South End (Harrison and Shawmut avenues near East Berkeley Street) had been transformed from a residential neighborhood into an unattractive industrial site. The West End, a poor neighborhood, at least remained residential, but its modest houses were razed and replaced by luxury housing. The South End's 616-acre renewal area—approximately one square mile—was physically the largest such project in the nation and culturally the most diverse. The city, having learned from its earlier mistakes, made a conscious effort to involve many different neighborhood groups in all the decisions that would affect their future.

Although the people living in the South End at the time could not have been happy with their neglected neighborhood, they still mistrusted what the city was about to do. The groups rejected several plans that would have meant the demolition of a large number of the South End's houses. Instead they supported efforts that provided loans and grants for those willing to undertake rehabilitation projects. The renewal plan that was finally accepted in 1965 focused on residential buildings, but it also included guidelines for preserving and reinforcing the positive, unifying, and unique qualities of the South End's street patterns, row houses, parks, and squares.

Fortunately the Boston Redevelopment Authority (BRA), the agency charged with administering Boston's urban renewal program, did not remove or destroy any of the historic garden features remaining in the squares. The original fountains in Blackstone and Franklin squares and Union Park and the fences around Union Park and Concord and Rutland squares were all left intact. In its effort to rehabilitate the gardens, the city was more interested in installing serviceable park furnishings that would make the gardens safer and more inviting than in acknowledging their history by providing period-style furnishings, which also may not have been readily available at the time.

In the late 1960s, the BRA installed eight contemporary "lollipop" lighting fixtures (hexagonal concrete poles with spherical white plastic globes) in each of Chester Square's gardens and replaced the chain-link fence with a plain black steel picket fence without finials. This relatively inexpensive type of fence was a modest improvement over the chain link but was only barely reminiscent of the elegant iron fence that had once graced Chester Square. In 1970, in an effort to upgrade Blackstone and Franklin squares, the city installed about thirty lollipop lighting fixtures in the garden of each square. Of the three youngest squares, Braddock Park was the only one improved by the BRA, which installed a concrete fountain between the two garden sections, a standard black steel picket fence, and lollipop lights.

Although the South End was considered a slum area when the neighborhood groups accepted the urban renewal plan, several hundred middle-class families had already recognized the benefits of living that close to downtown. Despite the difficulty in getting mortgages, these families saw the opportunity to restore Victorian row houses as a worthwhile challenge. Once the South End was declared an urban renewal project, mortgages became much easier to obtain. At around the same time, the Prudential Center was being developed as a large business and residential enclave directly to the northwest, across the railroad tracks in the Back Bay. The South End's proximity to the Back Bay and the Prudential Center did not go unnoticed. As more professionals moved into the area, many residents viewed them as people who would command more recognition by the city; others were afraid of being displaced.

Urban renewal was also accompanied by concern about the future of the nation's largest extant group of Victorian row houses. The urban renewal guidelines stipulated that only about 25 percent of the housing stock—the portion that was most deteriorated and was located along the area's major thoroughfares—would be demolished. In compliance with these guidelines, approximately three thousand row houses, situated primarily on the side streets, including the squares, were scheduled for rehabilitation. At the time the term "rehabilitation" meant simply that the houses would be repaired and refurbished, not necessarily restored to their former appearance. In 1966, recognizing that the urban renewal plan did not include any means of protecting the district's historic row houses, a group of residents founded the South End Historical Society, whose mission was to recognize and preserve the South End's historic resources. The society's first order of business was to educate current and prospective residents about the historic and aesthetic value of the row houses as well as to secure the protection of all buildings being rehabilitated under the urban renewal plan.

In 1973, after all the buildings in the district had been documented, the South End District was listed on the National Register of Historic Places as the largest urban Victorian neighborhood in the country, with an area of 238 acres, or about one-third of a square mile. This designation protected the historic exteriors of all buildings where rehabilitation by the public sector was to be partially funded by the federal government. A new tax credit, which applied only to buildings the private sector was rehabilitating for rental housing, also protected the exteriors. In 1977, the South End Historical Society petitioned the Boston Landmarks Commission (founded in 1975) for the creation of a South End Landmark District Commission. The society, concerned because the National Register listing did not protect renovation projects undertaken by individuals for their own use, hoped that a commission focused only on the South End would provide more comprehensive guidelines for restoring the exteriors of the area's historic buildings. Establishment of the South End Landmark District would take several years.

In 1979, the U.S. Department of Housing and Urban Development closed out all its urban renewal projects in Boston. By that time the growth in the number of middle- and upper-middle-class residents in the South End was well under way. Nevertheless, the South End still retained a proportionately high number of low-income families (45 percent) when compared to the city as a whole.

In 1983, after several years of study, the city officially designated over three hundred acres of the South End as a landmark district. Because the South End's large inventory of Victorian architecture had gone unrecognized for so long, it is not surprising that this designation was slow in coming—in fact, it occurred twenty-eight years after the Beacon Hill District Commission had been established and seventeen years after the Back Bay District Commission had been formed. The goals of the South End Landmark District Commission were to guide property owners in planning the rehabilitation of buildings and to help them determine which architectural changes were appropriate to the district. The district was rapidly becoming a magnet for middle-class residents, and there was an acute need to control the types of architectural changes that private owners made when upgrading and improving their properties.

According to the guidelines of the commission, its approval was required before any alterations could be made to the façades and the portions of roofs visible from the street on any property located within the boundaries of the landmark district. The intent of the specific standards and criteria established by the commission was to preserve the physical features, architectural character, and appearance of the South End, "a cohesive district of nineteenth-century Victorian red brick row houses." Any necessary changes were to be sensitive to the architectural character of the district, and intrusions were to be prevented. Major architectural categories covered by the guidelines included entrances, exterior walls, windows, roofs, fences, and yards.

By 1980, the most obvious sign that an economic revival was taking hold in the South End was the dramatic increase in the number of renovated row houses that exhibited elaborate exterior improvements. The new residents of the squares, who had been preoccupied with restoring their houses, were only just beginning to look beyond their front doors to the central gardens. The houses in all of the squares except Blackstone and Franklin had remained intact, thereby providing a potentially cohesive and concerned constituency for the gardens. In Chester Square, however, the residents were more preoccupied with pressing neighborhood issues, such as garbage and crime, than with the condition of the two narrow gardens outside their doors.

At this time Blackstone Square had original dwellings only on Shawmut Avenue and West Newton Street. The garden in Franklin Square was surrounded by the former St. James Hotel building, by then called the Franklin Square House (a home for the elderly) and the Cathedral Housing Project (a large affordable housing complex built in 1951). This complex was constructed on the East Brookline Street block fronting on Franklin Square where the Chilson houses had once stood. The noise and dirt created by the elevated railway still running between Blackstone and Franklin squares continued to cast a pall over an already depressed area. Despite a relatively small constituency for their very large gardens, a group of new residents was motivated to form the Blackstone/Franklin Squares Neighborhood Association (B/FSNA) to address both the social problems affecting their neighborhood and the deteriorated gardens.

Undaunted by the alcoholics and drug addicts who frequented the gardens, the residents—who soon became committed to rescuing the gardens and making them as safe and welcoming as possible—began to lobby the city for improvements. In the early 1980s, with funding from three sources (Community Development Block Grant, the federal Land and Water Conservation Fund, and the city's Edward Ingersoll Browne Fund), Blackstone and Franklin squares underwent a major facelift. A new steel picket fence with cast-iron tulip-shaped finials was installed around each garden. Because new lighting fixtures had been installed as recently as 1970, a decision was made to save money and not replace these fixtures with the popular "historic-style" lights, which had acorn-shaped globes. The two original fountains, which had become rusted hulks, were completely refurbished but were not converted to re-circulating fountains, which were not yet mandatory in Boston. The existing concrete and wood benches, then in total disrepair, were replaced with ten cast-iron and wood Victorian-style benches in each garden. During this restoration the tree stock, which had been depleted by one-half in the roughly ten years since 1970, was replenished with new linden trees, bringing the total number of trees to fifty-four in Blackstone Square and sixty-five in Franklin Square—or about half the number of trees originally planted in the mid-nineteenth century. Although the new trees filled in some of the gaps, they were not plentiful enough to clearly define the paths and grass areas—particularly along the perimeters of the garden, which had been the intent in the original design.

The BRA, acting in response to pressure from the Park Committee of the Worcester Square Neighborhood Association, next reconstructed the garden in Worcester Square. Starting in the 1960s the square's residents had kept their garden closed except for special events, such as their annual Christmas tree-lighting ceremony. The central path had been removed, but five large elm trees, each three feet in diameter, still remained, as did the original carved granite fountain basin—identical to the two in Union Park—and most of the granite bases for the original fence. The residents had informally embellished the garden with flowers, shrubs, and a fir tree at each end. In 1984, a landscape architect from the Boston Redevelopment Authority was assigned the task of working with the community to redesign the garden and raise funds for its reconstruction. The entire project was funded by the city's Edward Ingersoll Browne Fund and the George B. Henderson Foundation—both of which supported local beautification efforts—as well as by the city of Boston's capital fund.

Although the South End Landmark District Commission's primary responsibility was overseeing architectural improvements, it became very involved in the redesign of Worcester Square. Because of budget constraints and community input, the commission did not insist that the garden be restored to its nineteenth-century appearance. A reproduction of the original Louisburg Square–style fence would have been too expensive, so a simpler custom-made fence was designed, reviewed, and modified by the commission during meetings held over the course of several months. Rather than having the original nineteenth-century fountain reproduced, the community chose a local sculptor to design a contemporary-style fountain depicting two women and two children. The original basin, measuring fifteen feet in diameter, was removed and replaced with a basin approximately twenty-five feet in diameter. Unlike the fountains in Union Park,

where the original statues have never been replaced, the inclusion of a decorative sculpture captured the spirit—if not the actual appearance—of Worcester Square's original fountain.

Issues such as whether to include a central path and line it with benches were discussed at length by the community and the commission. These issues were controversial because the community was more interested in discouraging use of the garden than in restoring it to its original appearance. The final design included a central path but no benches. In fact, the earliest photographs of the garden do not show benches, although early-twentieth-century images do. The community also decided against restoring the original width of the garden, which had been narrowed by seven feet on each side in 1957 in order to make the streets wider for cars.

The plantings, too, were a contemporary adaptation of the garden's nineteenth-century design. Four pagoda trees and four plane trees were planted to protect against the loss of all the trees if one species were affected by disease in the future. Some large elms (which occupied a lot of space) still remained. The new trees increased to nine the number of trees on each side of the garden, versus twelve on each side when the garden was originally planted. In addition to grass and trees, the new design included a five-foot-wide flowerbed

Worcester Square, 2001.

Depicting two women with children, the sculpture of Worcester Square's fountain stands on a granite pedestal in the center of a basin that is ten feet wider than the square's original basin. The tree in the upper right-hand corner is a pagoda tree planted during the 1990 reconstruction.

encircling the fountain basin with rose bushes that were reminiscent of the garden's early decorative plantings.

The improvement of Union Park started out in much the same way as it did in Worcester Square but ultimately took a different direction. Beginning in the 1960s, the Union Park Association had been actively involved in caring for the grass and planting flowers and trees. Although the gardens in Union Park and Worcester Square looked quite similar during the 1970s and 1980s, there were some significant differences. Both had flowering shrubs, unkempt yews and spruces, occasional patches of flowers, and no central path; but Union Park's garden was still surrounded by its early-twentieth-century fence and contained its two original fountains, although they were missing their original cast-iron sculptures. With these important historical features in place, in the mid-1980s the Union Park Association sought and received the South End Landmark District Commission's permission to add four cast-iron urns, which corresponded closely to those in a 1916 photo.

Stewardship and Restoration

By the 1990s, the South End, having undergone the exhausting process of urban renewal followed by economic revival and redevelopment, was ready for a period of relative stability. Although the urban renewal process had entailed public control of much of the housing rehabilitation, the influx of more affluent homeowners brought with it a shift in control to the private sector. Once the houses in the squares had been renovated, their owners began to lobby for more public support of the gardens, in part to enhance the value of their real estate. The residents believed that because the gardens were owned by the city, it was the city's obligation to accept the burden of any necessary capital repairs as well as ongoing maintenance. The residents did not mind taking on some of the simple gardening tasks, such as weeding flowerbeds and planting shrubs, but without the city's participation the gardens in Union Park and Worcester Square ended up looking more like unplanned private yards than public historic landscapes.

In the cases of privately owned gardens—for instance, Louisburg Square in Boston, Gramercy Park in New York City, and initially all of London's squares—it was traditional for the owners to manage and maintain their gardens, usually without any help from the city. On the other hand, residents living in squares with publicly owned gardens were not obligated to care for the gardens even though individually they might be very interested in high standards of upkeep and appearance. The early 1990s marked the beginning of "public/ private partnerships," a marriage of the public and private sectors in which the two shared responsibilities for managing and maintaining public open spaces, regardless of whether they were historic landscapes. The role of the residents was to serve as private stewards who would work with the city to delineate shared responsibilities. In the South End, such a partnership had the potential to ensure the successful maintenance and preservation of the squares.

In creating this type of relationship, the greatest challenge for South End residents was to forge a strong partnership with the city— the owner of the gardens—that was based on mutual trust and each partner's understanding of the needs and resources of the other. Both partners needed to agree that these gardens were historic landscapes that should be treated accordingly. Since maintenance and restoration of these gardens required substantial funding, it would have been ideal if the city had been able to commit sufficient resources to completely restore and care for the gardens. Unfortunately, not only were the city's resources insufficient but the residents in the South End squares were unable to supplement public sector funding, except on a very limited basis in Union Park. There, during the late 1990s, the newly formed Friends of Union Park began to contract privately for all landscaping tasks—lawn work, flower planting, and fountain and irrigation repairs.

In the case of Blackstone and Franklin squares, the gardens were too large for the small constituency to take on financial responsibility for their care. Fortunately, in 1991 these two squares, as well as Worcester Square, received a special ten-year linkage grant for neighborhood improvements from Boston University Medical Associates (BUMA), when BUMA was seeking community approval for its nearby BioSquare project. As a result, between 1991 and 2001 the gardens in Blackstone, Franklin, and Worcester squares benefited greatly from the private BUMA grants, which were used for fountain improvements, tree pruning, and, in Worcester Square, the installation of an irrigation system. Without the infusion of private monies, these gardens would have begun to deteriorate. There had been discussion of earmarking some of the funds as seed money for a maintenance endowment before the grant ran out, and as a result, seventy thousand dollars in unspent funds went directly to the Blackstone and Franklin Squares Neighborhood Association. The association was then faced with the daunting challenge of raising enough additional money to bring the endowment up to a level that could support the maintenance of the gardens.

What the residents of all the squares did not provide in dollars they more than made up for in hours of volunteer services in maintaining their gardens. The residents had taken on the traditional role of stewards of their gardens as early as the 1960s. After their gardens were restored in the early 1980s, a few residents of Blackstone and Franklin squares volunteered their time for such maintenance tasks as pruning new trees, which were still small enough to reach easily, oiling the new benches, and cleaning the fountain basins. When the city agreed to fund the 1990 restoration plan for Union Park, it required a formal maintenance agreement between the Boston Parks Department and the Union Park Association, outlining the responsibilities of both parties. The Parks Department agreed to fund the same types of fountain repairs in Union Park, when money was available, that the BUMA grant covered in Blackstone, Franklin, and Worcester squares. The residents of Union Park and Worcester Square devoted many hours to cleaning the fountains and caring for the new flowerbeds, while the Parks Department provided standard services—for example, mowing grass, removing tree stumps, and occasionally pruning trees.

The controversial issue of access to the gardens, which had arisen during the economic revival of the 1980s, intensified during the stewardship period of the 1990s. The gardens in the South End squares were different from private squares because—since their inception—the city had been both their creator and their owner. Because the gardens in Blackstone and Franklin squares were so large, they had always been open for everyone to enjoy. However, during the mid-nineteenth century the residents of Chester Square had keys to their garden, which they kept locked. Nineteenth-century photographs of Union Park and Worcester Square show the gates in these squares both open and closed, and so the two gardens may not have actually been locked, or at least not all the time.

Although most of the funds for the reconstruction of Worcester Square in the 1980s had come from the public sector, Worcester Square's Park Committee, which initially had intended to keep the garden open, quickly decided to keep the gates locked to protect the garden from damage. The residents of Union Park also decided to privatize their garden by keeping the gates locked except on special occasions. The city's Parks Department chose not to interfere with these decisions, even though many people believed that landscapes supported by public funds should be kept accessible. On the other hand, it is easy to understand why the residents, who had taken a proprietary interest in the care of these small, historic landscapes enclosed by their signature fences, chose to lock the gates. Gated gardens, even when intended to be open to all, lend themselves to privatization.

The informal public/private partnerships evolved as the private stewards sought and received funds for the redesign of Worcester Square during the 1980s and for the maintenance of the gardens in

Blackstone, Franklin, and Worcester squares during the 1990s. However, these partnerships did not focus on restoring the gardens as historic landscapes. In the case of Worcester Square, where neither of the garden's original signature features—the fence and fountain—remained, the final design was a contemporary interpretation of the nineteenth-century garden. Cost issues, particularly the expense of a reproduction cast-iron fence, might have influenced the decision not to restore Worcester Square's garden to its mid-nineteenth-century appearance. Although the South End Landmark District Commission's standards and criteria for rehabilitating buildings encouraged the appropriate restoration of private dwellings, the publicly owned gardens in the squares also were in need of preservation guidelines.

Several years after the 1983 designation of the South End as a landmark district, the Union Park Association began to focus its efforts on restoring the garden to its original appearance. Working without the benefit of guidelines for historic landscapes, the association had to rely on consensus, based primarily on residents' personal views. Funds for the 1990 restoration plan came from the city's Browne Fund and the private Henderson Foundation. In addition, the Henderson Foundation offered a challenge grant of fifty thousand dollars toward a new Louisburg Square–style fence, which resembled the original fence. The restoration committee was unsuccessful in raising the necessary matching funds, however, and the project was postponed. By the end of the 1990s, with the existing fence in great need of repairs, the association again sought funding for a new fence, although by this time many of the residents wanted to reproduce or repair the current fence rather than to reproduce the original one. Cost considerations played a large part in this decision, but the residents also justified their choice on the grounds of height; they preferred the height of the existing four-foot picket fence to the height of the original five-foot lotus-stalk fence.

An important part of the restoration plan involved rehabilitating the two original fountains, which had greatly deteriorated, and installing new pumps and large underground holding tanks for re-circulating water. Because the residents may have been unaware that each of the fountain vases originally had been embellished with a statue of Leda and the Swan, there was no attempt to introduce sculptures. Unlike the Worcester Square community, the Union Park residents chose not to restore the garden's original central path, which had been planted with grass in the 1970s, because they wished the garden to be viewed rather than used. This decision was inconsistent with the more conventional preservation treatment of restoring the original form of a landscape when features (fountains, in this case) still exist from that period. The new plan proposed relocating several existing

Union Park, 2001.

The foreground of this photograph shows Union Park's 1903 fence, which replaced the original lotus-stalk fence and was identical to the fence in Chester Square and around Concord Square's fountain, both of which were installed at about the same time. The trees are lindens planted during the 1992 restoration of the garden.

lindens and planting four new ones, bringing the total number of trees to twenty-two (eleven on each side of the garden), a configuration that was quite similar to the original twelve elms on each side. The lawn was re-graded, an irrigation system was installed, a new flagpole was set on a granite base, and sod was laid.

During the mid-1990s, while the residents of Blackstone and Franklin squares were using their BUMA grants to maintain the fountains and trees, they were also working with the Parks Department to obtain a major U.S. Transportation Department grant to restore the gardens to their nineteenth-century appearance. The gardens were eligible for this grant because of their location on a major thoroughfare, Washington Street. Although the residents were very disappointed when this grant did not materialize, the complicated application process, which required many support letters, focused new attention on these historically significant landscapes. The grant money would have been used to restore many of the gardens' original features. For example, a replica of the original, elaborate cast-iron fence would have been installed, and the modern asphalt paths would have been returned to their original stone dust surface. In addition, the funds would have been used to eliminate the major drainage problems in the lawn areas so that more trees could have been planted successfully, and to convert the original fountains to re-circulating systems. Without the grant, the only improvements the city made to these gardens in the late 1990s were completing the planting of street trees around Blackstone Square and installing acorn-style lighting fixtures to replace the inappropriate lollipop-style lights.

In 1952, Chester Square had been split by the intrusion of Massachusetts Avenue. Forty-two years later, when the city announced that it planned to improve Massachusetts Avenue, the residents of Chester Square took advantage of the opportunity to try to realize their dream of reuniting the two gardens. With a small service grant from the National Trust for Historic Preservation, the residents hired a private consultant, who worked with the Parks Department to engage the community in a planning process that included a design charrette to help create a vision for a newly restored garden. As an interim gesture, the city installed several benches and reproduction cast-iron urns. Working with the city, the Chester Square residents were eventually successful in securing a grant from the Massachusetts Highway Department to assess the feasibility of constructing an underpass between Tremont Street and Shawmut Avenue, thereby knitting the two gardens back together. The study determined that an underpass was physically feasible but would cost an estimated $7 million to construct. The project, which was competing with other local

Blackstone Square, 2001.

This view of Blackstone Square shows its original fountain, which is operating but—for safety reasons—is not pumping out enough water to fill the basin. Mature lindens form an *allée* of trees along one path, and maple trees with maroon-colored leaves planted along West Newton Street compensate for the lack of trees within the garden at this edge.

transportation projects that the city was considering for other neighborhoods, eventually died.

The city has been more successful in implementing landscape restoration projects in the smaller squares with the help of its Browne Fund and the Henderson Foundation. In its effort to bring all the squares up to a "consistent level of quality," the Parks Department worked with the residents of the three smallest squares during the late 1990s to fund desired restoration projects. These projects included repairing the fences around the gardens of Concord and Rutland squares; replacing Concord Square's original fountain and its surrounding fence; replanting the gardens with grass or groundcover, depending on the wishes of the residents; and installing acorn-style lights and hose bibs for watering the plantings.

By the summer of 2002, the city had worked with the residents of Braddock Park, located between Columbus Avenue and what is now the Southwest Corridor Park, to introduce some garden features that would make the late-1960s design appear more traditional. Although there is no evidence that the garden ever had a cast-iron fountain, a small, period-style cast-iron fountain on a pedestal—with a verdigris finish—was placed in an oval granite basin, and round black finials were attached to the tops of the black steel fence posts. Probably for cost reasons, the large, rough-cut granite posts from the late-1960s fence were not replaced.

Franklin Square, 2001.

This photo of Franklin Square shows its tree canopy, which is denser than that of Blackstone Square. Most of the lindens pictured were planted in the early 1980s, although a much older linden can be seen at the left. Acorn lighting fixtures were installed recently, but oil drums are still used as trash receptacles.

Chester Square, 2001.

In order to show both sides of Chester Square, this photo was taken when there was no traffic on Massachusetts Avenue. The twin brownstone houses on the south side of the square are visible through the oak trees planted in the late 1960s, when the lollipop lights and the plain black steel fencing were also installed.

Concord Square, 2001.

This photograph of Concord Square shows the new two-tiered cast-iron fountain that replaced the original lotus-flower fountain vase. The earlier vase was identical to the Union Park fountain vases but could not be repaired. Two cast-iron urns for flowers are planned for each of the two garden sections.

Despite efforts on the part of both the public and the private sectors to carry out small-scale restoration projects in some of the squares, major garden restoration projects for Blackstone, Franklin, and Chester squares were no longer being considered.

Because the South End consists primarily of restored brick row houses, the casual visitor is unlikely to stumble on the gardens in any of the squares. The five smallest ones—Union and Braddock parks together with Worcester, Concord, and Rutland squares—are well hidden by their enclosing buildings. The original row houses still remain in Chester Square, but its gardens are barely visible to the

Rutland Square, 2001.

This photograph shows the first of the three sections comprising Rutland Square's garden, with the Venetian-Gothic-style houses on the left. The early fence, except for the end shown in this view, was removed but has since been repaired, painted, and reinstalled. The garden sections are planted with periwinkle and ivy groundcover.

thousands of drivers who speed through it along Massachusetts Avenue every day. Although the gardens of Blackstone and Franklin squares are the largest and most exposed, they are located in a section of the South End that has until now attracted few visitors from outside the neighborhood.

Those who deliberately seek out the South End squares are usually surprised to find that all the gardens, except those in Chester Square, are well maintained and still functioning as passive landscapes for sitting or viewing. All are surrounded by black fences—some quite old, but not original. Colorful perennial borders around each of the two fountains now grace Union Park, and Worcester Square has a circle of rose bushes. Noting the care that has been lavished on these gardens, the visitor would probably assume they are privately owned, especially because their gates are locked. Even Blackstone and Franklin squares, where many of the original dwellings have disappeared, compensate for this loss with their many trees, benches, and the original dolphin fountains that spray water in the summer heat.

The *New York Times* has described the present-day South End as having "gracious Victorian houses, gardens, hidden parks, bistros and a human *mélange* of races, classes and occupations." It is precisely these features that, to the dismay of some, are contributing to an increase in real estate values and a growing middle-class presence. Yet the South End continues to have a very large group of protected affordable housing developments. Some people, however, believe it is important to attract people with incomes high enough so that they can invest in their properties and neighborhood. The South End is currently attracting a group of middle-class residents—suburban empty nesters as well as families with young children—who, as has been mentioned, are in many respects similar to the people the city tried to attract with its garden squares in the mid-nineteenth century. Union Park has become the trophy neighborhood of the South End, offering a convenient location, expensive housing, and a well-manicured, locked garden that the residents treat as their own.

Although the garden squares of the South End are noteworthy in that most of their buildings are intact and restored, each of the gardens is at a different stage in the restoration process. As a result of recent improvements, the landscape features of all the squares have been stabilized to include trees and grass—the traditional plant materials of a garden square—and occasional flowers. Throughout their long history the two largest gardens—those of Blackstone and Franklin squares—have also managed to preserve their original passive uses as places for strolling and sitting, despite the fact that in recent years they have also served as sites for more active programming, for instance, concerts and festivals. Strolling and sitting have been elimi-

Braddock Park, 2001.

Since this photograph of Braddock Park was taken, efforts have been made to upgrade the 1960s reconstruction. Round finials have been added atop the steel fence posts, and a small, period-style cast-iron fountain in an oval granite basin has replaced the modern concrete fountain that had been situated between the two garden sections.

nated in the gardens of Union Park and Worcester Square, and these two gardens now function solely as places to be viewed.

The overall integrity of the gardens in all of the South End's squares except Chester Square has been preserved because of the public sector's benign neglect of a declining neighborhood for a hundred years, followed by major financial assistance from that same public sector during the past thirty years. This situation is markedly different from Louisburg Square, where the garden's preservation has been solely the result of constant care and attention by the private sector. In most instances, except for urban renewal projects, city-financed improvements to the gardens have come as a result of pressure from the private sector. Because all the gardens in the South End squares have remained publicly owned spaces, the residents have never really been in a position to control the level of resources—funds or services—that the city chooses to commit toward restoring these gardens.

Preservation efforts in the squares will continue to ebb and flow in response to changes in the city's economy and political leadership as well as in the amount of time and energy the residents are able to devote to lobbying the city on behalf of their historic landscapes. If the residents or their neighborhood organizations were in a stronger financial position, they might be able to leverage more services from the city. Yet when Blackstone and Franklin squares were beneficiaries of the ten-year BUMA grant, the city chose not to supplement the grant with increased municipal services for these two very large gardens, which had a great many needs.

London Squares Revisited

The evolution of the South End's garden squares and London's Bloomsbury squares had much in common, although in London's squares the terrace houses did not fare as well as the South End's row houses. At the end of the nineteenth century, when the London City Council removed the gates of the Bloomsbury Estate, the Bloomsbury district became accessible to the public, although its gardens were still privately owned. As property leases expired, the estate owner either offered repairing leases (according to which a new lessee was required to implement specific repairs and improvements), demolished buildings, or sold property to commercial interests and to such institutions as the British Museum and the University of London. Some of the single-family residences were converted to multi-family dwellings, just as they were in the South End, but many of the terrace houses became offices, hotels, or residences for students.

In London, the middle classes moved out to the newer suburbs, and a more heterogeneous population moved to the squares. The new occupants—whether full-time residents or daytime office workers—were not very interested in caring for the gardens. Except for the garden in Bedford Square, which remained well tended even though all its original terrace houses had become offices, the gardens in Bloomsbury began to deteriorate. The gardens in the South End squares, which also had deteriorated (because the city had neglected them for almost a century), had managed to retain a few of their original fountains, the 1913 fences in Concord and Rutland squares, and the early-twentieth-century fence in Union Park. It was precisely the fences—or "railings," as they were commonly called—that played a pivotal role in the fate of London's squares.

During World War II, when almost all the fences were taken down for use as scrap metal, London's squares suffered a major threat to their integrity. This "de-railing" of the gardens turned out to have a profound effect on their future. When the iron railings were first offered up voluntarily and then were requisitioned, there was much discussion in the London press about the pros and cons of sacrificing these historic landscape furnishings. Some viewed railings as symbols of entitlement and the rights to privacy and property whereas others considered them exclusionary and antidemocratic. In some respects these reactions were comparable to those of the South End residents when confronted with the prospect of urban renewal: they were afraid that once the neighborhood had been improved, it would become gentrified. Despite some dissension, the trustees of St. James's Square voluntarily removed their fence in 1941 but replaced it with a temporary wooden one. On the Bloomsbury Estate, the railings of Russell and Bloomsbury squares were voluntarily removed. (Financial remuneration for the scrap metal usually was given to the estate owner, who in all probability had paid for the railings in the first place.) However, the estate office was permitted to keep the railing in Bedford Square because of its "historic value," which was probably a way of rewarding the estate for taking such good care of the garden for so many years.

After the war not only the estate owners but also London's citizenry in general were forced to reevaluate the role of these historic landscapes, which had been exclusive, private gardens for so long. The immediate result of the widespread removal of railings from squares throughout London was that the formerly private gardens were now completely accessible to the public. Suddenly the owners of these exclusive enclaves could no longer control either the numbers of visitors to their gardens or the amount of wear-and-tear that would ensue. Residents questioned whether they were still obligated to pay rates (fees) for the maintenance of gardens that were now accessible to the public. As has been mentioned, the trustees of St. James's Square erected a temporary wooden fence around their garden, and temporary fences—made of wood or chain link—were also installed in other squares. The Bloomsbury Estate took the opportunity to divest itself of several of its squares. In 1943, the estate gave Russell and Bloomsbury squares to the Borough of Holborn (now Camden) to manage, and in 1950 and 1951, the estate sold Tavistock and Gordon squares to the Borough of St. Pancras and Torrington and Woburn squares to the University of London. Of Bloomsbury's seven squares, only Bedford Square's garden, with its original fence still intact, remained both locked and under estate ownership.

During the fifty-year period following this dramatic shift from private to public management or ownership of many of the gardens, one could deduce that certain squares were publicly maintained because they were generally less well cared for than the private squares. Although starting in the late 1980s new railings began to be installed in some gardens, it was not until 1995—the fiftieth anniversary of the end of World War II and five years before the Millennium—that the squares became the object of renewed attention. Local authorities and resident groups attempted to raise money through lotteries for new railings. That year the London Historic Parks and Gardens Trust initiated and organized the London Squares Conference: A Forum on the Past, Present and Future of London's Squares. The purpose of this conference was to raise public awareness of the squares and to encourage action in several areas—legal protection, creation of an updated inventory, fundraising, and the preparation of management and restoration plans. The fact that some of the goals of the conference have been achieved over the past few years has important implications for Boston, which has yet to provide a forum for evaluating the status of its garden squares.

Several legal issues continue to pose major problems for the management of London's squares, regardless of whether this is by the private or public sector. The London Squares Preservation Act of 1931, which protected 461 squares, failed to protect the subsoil beneath squares, with the unfortunate result that underground parking garages have already been built under some squares such as Bloomsbury Square. Others can still be built. Another problem involves the collection of money to maintain the gardens in some squares. Although appropriate legislation exists regarding the collection of money, many taxpayers whose property overlooks a garden do not pay their assessments. Those who do pay are concerned that the gardens will not receive proper care and will deteriorate if others do not pay.

Many landscape maintenance problems that arise in connection with caring for London's gardens are similar to those confronted by both the public and private stewards of Boston's squares. With tree care as the major concern, the consensus is that mature trees that are too big or not healthy should be removed. More diverse species of trees should be planted so that an entire tree population is not wiped out if a particular disease strikes. There is an urgent need for management and landscape plans with recommendations for suitable plantings and materials for pathways. Since London's garden squares are, for the most part, much larger than Boston's, such issues as appropriate play equipment and the advisability of hosting events requiring catering and entertainment are also of concern. Not surprisingly, the subject of railings is important, and recommendations range from reconstructing the original style of railings to instituting new styles of railing design. Restoring the gardens to a particular historical period does not seem to be a priority for those entrusted with caring for them. Instead, the emphasis in London is on preserving the unique character of each garden.

As a result of the 1995 conference, several important projects have begun recently relating to the improvement of the gardens in the squares. Although a pan-London bid for lottery funding failed through lack of support from the London boroughs, several individual squares have received lottery money. Russell Square's garden, the centerpiece of the Duke of Bedford's Bloomsbury Estate and (at ten acres) London's largest, was recently rehabilitated with money from the Heritage Lottery Fund. Although the original fence and 1804 layout by Humphry Repton, England's foremost landscape designer during that period, were restored, the café and central fountains, which had been added in 1960, were replaced with contemporary-style furnishings. The new fountain, which represents a clock, has twelve water jets that emerge from a shallow pool flush with the ground. The new café includes a snack bar, restaurant, and children's activity rooms. This preservation treatment probably would qualify as a "rehabilitation," which is discussed in the next section.

The London Historic Parks and Gardens Trust assisted the London Gardens Society in organizing the 1997 London Squares Competition, which has become an annual event. In 1998, London Garden Squares Day was inaugurated. This event is an initiative of the trust in collaboration with English Heritage, the government's principal adviser on the protection of England's historic environment. The goal of this annual June event is "to raise awareness of the diversity and beauty of garden squares scattered throughout London and draw attention to the great contribution which these green spaces make to the capital and the importance attached to their conservation." Starting with forty-three squares, which attracted more than two thousand visitors, by 2002 the number of participating squares had grown to about seventy-five.

Another outgrowth of the 1995 conference was the publication in 1996 of *Garden Square News*. This independently published magazine provides a forum for the exchange of information among the individuals who manage and use the "communal gardens" (as the private gardens are often called) in Chelsea, Kensington, and Westminster. The subjects covered include all the predictable maintenance and horticultural issues that are also common to Boston's garden squares as well as more controversial issues—for instance, building underground parking garages, introducing playground equipment and sculptures into the gardens, and using the gardens as movie sets. The problem of how to fund replacement railings is also the subject of much discussion.

Articles in *Garden Square News* reflect the significant change in ownership of the gardens during recent years. Whereas historically all gardens were owned by an estate, the landlords (who were forbidden to build on—and often beneath—them) are now anxious to relieve themselves of the financial burden of caring for their gardens. Although the leaseholders or residents traditionally have been assessed a "rate" or fee that covered many of the expenses, the estate has often had to supplement these monies. There has been much discussion about whether the private garden committees or the boroughs are better equipped to own and manage the gardens that the estate owners relinquish. When an estate has allowed the garden committee to purchase the garden it oversees, there is still the question of who is in the best position to enforce the collection of rates, because garden committees are rarely successful in collecting from everyone. There are still other advantages in giving control to the boroughs: they may have more political clout in resisting the pressure of developers, and they are better qualified to solicit grants from the lottery and from private sources that prefer to fund gardens that are open and accessible to the public.

In 2000, through its Campaign for London Squares, English Heritage began to take a leadership role in trying to raise awareness and funds for the protection of London's approximately six hundred squares. Acknowledging that squares represent a unique blend of "built and landscaped form, uniformity and diversity and public and private territory" that has shaped London for over three hundred years, this campaign outlined the following benefits that the squares continue to provide. Socially, squares in residential neighborhoods foster a community spirit through the use of shared space, the work of garden committee members, and the provision of an area where children can play safely. In business areas squares serve as green oases where office workers can meet and relax. Visually, squares are welcome interruptions in the dense urban fabric, making the city more livable and human in scale. As home to trees, plants, and wildlife, squares are also a link to the natural world with its changing seasons.

It is not surprising that English Heritage, in its role as statutory advisor to the government, supports only those gardens that are open to the public. Yet in the case of Bedford Square, the campaign has provided money to reinstate the original layout of the square's sidewalks and carriageways, which are open to the public, even though the garden remains private. In serving as a catalyst for the enhancement of London's squares and the increase in public access to them, the organization has pledged to work in partnership with the mayor, the London boroughs, estates, companies, trusts, and private donors to raise money for the project. In addition, English Heritage will contribute up to £200,000 in challenge grants for the installation of railings modeled on the original patterns in prominent squares that have appropriate public access. English Heritage has also committed to providing free professional and technical assistance to groups that are responsible for the upkeep of the gardens. The Campaign for London Squares has stressed the importance of attractive and well-managed squares both for the city's residents and for its 25,000,000 annual visitors.

Although Boston's South End has a very small number of garden squares compared to London, it is still possible for Boston's garden stewards—both public and private—to use English Heritage as a model in creating an effective process for restoring and protecting their squares. The social, visual, environmental, and economic benefits of squares as articulated by English Heritage for London are essentially the same for Boston. Even though the South End is a residential neighborhood, it has the potential to be a tourist attraction in Boston. Whereas English Heritage supports public access to London squares, the South End squares are already owned by the city. For the squares in both cities, money—and how to find it—is, as always, the greatest challenge.

Preservation Strategies

The South End's garden squares have managed to retain much of their integrity over the years. Because these gardens retain older fences and original fountains, and are too small to have had many new accretions, interest in restoring them to their nineteenth-century appearance has been greater than has been true with the squares in London. Nevertheless, even though the gardens of Blackstone and Franklin squares are the largest and, therefore, have the potential to serve the greatest number of South End residents, they receive relatively little attention from the city. While the South End Landmark District Commission has not established guidelines to prescribe appropriate preservation treatments for the gardens in the squares, such guidelines for historic landscapes now exist at the federal level.

The *Guidelines for the Treatment of Cultural Landscapes*, which was published by the U.S. National Park Service in 1996, addresses four treatments for preserving historic landscapes—preservation, rehabilitation, restoration, and reconstruction. Preservation, the most rigorous of the four treatments, not only assumes that a particular landscape has retained most of its original fabric but also requires that when its forms and features have evolved over time, these changes should also be kept. Rehabilitation, while also requiring that a landscape's historic character be retained, permits adaptations for contemporary uses. The goal of restoration is to take a landscape back to a particular historical period even if this treatment entails removing the accretions from other periods. Finally, the least rigorous treatment from a conceptual point of view is reconstruction or the re-creation of a now-vanished landscape with new materials. Just as with restoration, reconstruction attempts to return a landscape to its most significant period.

In the absence of local guidelines, efforts to improve the gardens of the South End squares have reflected a variety of informal treatments. Worcester Square's garden was reconstructed because there was no effort to save its original fountain basin, and great liberties were taken with the fountain design. If Chester Square's garden were ever improved, it too would necessitate reconstruction because none of its historic features remain. Although Union Park has the potential to meet stricter preservation standards, because it retains an old—though not original—fence as well as parts of the original fountains, a consensus has not yet been reached on what action to take. Some would like to restore the garden to its nineteenth-century appearance by bringing back the original lotus-stalk fence and the original path, whereas others are happy with the early-twentieth-century fence. By allowing the gates of Union Park and Worcester Square to be locked, making the gardens accessible only to volunteer workers, the city has perpetuated the still-unresolved issue of privatizing these gardens. Yet, as has been shown, this type of privatization may also have occurred soon after the gardens were created in the nineteenth century.

Although the National Park Service guidelines are a good resource for choosing the appropriate preservation treatment for large, historic landscapes such as municipal parks, they do not provide a systematic approach for dealing with a family of relatively small urban landscapes such as garden squares. The South End squares have survived as a group of related landscapes for at least 150 years without losing their original forms or even their original purpose as passive green spaces, and most of them are still surrounded by their nineteenth-century buildings. As with many of London's garden squares, the South End squares have begun to function as small parks serving the immediate neighborhood, thereby demonstrating their flexibility and usefulness over time.

Because all landscapes continue to evolve as a result of natural processes (in addition to the human activities to which they are subjected), perhaps preservation is the most appropriate treatment for many historic landscapes, even though this type of treatment requires more careful deliberation than restoration. But in the case of the South End's squares, where both the nineteenth-century row houses and the gardens are still intact, it seems appropriate that many of their stewards have opted to restore the gardens to their nineteenth-century appearance. Just as important as choosing precisely how to restore the gardens, however, is acknowledging that managing and maintaining them through effective public/private partnerships is essential to their long-term viability as historic landscapes. It is also essential that a program be developed for interpreting the South End's garden squares as representing a significant urban landscape form that was transplanted from London and pre-dated the well-known Olmsted parks of Boston. Information comparing the privately owned Louisburg Square, which everyone admires, to the South End's public garden squares, which few people know about, should be widely disseminated. Undoubtedly a greater understanding and appreciation of these landscapes by the public at large will eventually result in increased funding for their upkeep.

The South End needs to create a catalyst, an organization that is committed to raising awareness of the squares and to advocating for the funding to restore and enhance their gardens. English Heritage's statement about London garden squares could easily apply to squares in the South End: "Squares are a unique and essential part of London's townscape. At their best they effect a seamless unification of architecture, street plan and open space. They are crucially important focal points in the public realm." A South End squares conservancy made up of residents and friends of the South End could at least begin to promote awareness of these historic landscapes. A conservancy would provide not only an opportunity for residents of the entire South End to rally around the cause of protecting the gardens in all the squares but could also serve as a forum for residents to share the expertise they have already acquired in maintaining their trees and fountains. Members of this group could convene regularly with representatives of the Parks Department to determine priorities and draw up an action plan for the entire group of squares. The Parks Department has always dealt with the squares individually in response to pressure from residents of a particular square. The conservancy, representing a much larger constituency, would be in a stronger position to prioritize needs so that the squares with the most vocal residents do not continue to receive preferential treatment. Ultimately the goal of the conservancy would be to advocate and raise funds for improvements to all the gardens.

The story of the planning of Boston's South End garden squares reveals that the gardens in these squares initially were similar to their London prototypes in all respects except that they were laid out by the city and consequently were not privately owned. In terms of managing, maintaining, and preserving the gardens, public ownership of these spaces has proved to be a challenge over the years. After the houses in the squares were restored, the residents began to take more of an interest in the gardens. Although the private stewards in the South End have often volunteered their time for the upkeep of their gardens, they have never been able to dedicate their own funds to the task or find other private funding for the gardens.

Because the South End garden squares are a unique feature of a landmark district that is the largest urban Victorian residential neighborhood in the United States, a special effort must be made to avoid focusing on its buildings to the exclusion of these historic landscapes. Few people realize just how similar these squares are to those of London and, even more important, what a unique treasure—a family of intact garden squares—is hidden in the South End. Just as in the mid-nineteenth century the city invested time and money in planning and furnishing the gardens in the South End squares, today it has an obligation to allocate those same resources for preserving the gardens as a significant legacy for the use and appreciation of future generations.

CONCLUSION

$\mathcal{T}$HE GARDEN SQUARES of both London and Boston have, over a long period of time, demonstrated their viability as an urban landscape form. The garden square was introduced in London in the mid-seventeenth century as a new type of speculative real estate venture featuring a garden as its centerpiece. In the late eighteenth century, the garden square was transplanted to Boston, where it was used for essentially the same purpose. These historic urban landscapes, having successfully served as magnets for builders and residents, lasted well beyond their formative stage and are still flourishing in both cities. Garden squares are not the anachronisms that some might believe them to be. They have functioned as intended despite changing social, economic, and political conditions in two countries and on two continents. They owe their longevity primarily to the fact that since their inception the gardens have served as passive green spaces for their abutters, who have taken a proprietary interest in their care.

As many mercantile cities became increasingly crowded during the middle of the nineteenth century, citizens and social reformers demanded large parks as relief from the oppressive dirt and congestion that engulfed the downtown areas. By the second half of the century, London and Boston each boasted at least one large municipal park that served as a welcome refuge for the general public. Yet these parks did not replace the small garden squares that had already been developed in each city. The residents of each square had paid a premium to live where they could look out on an attractive garden and enjoy strolling or sitting amid grass, trees, and flowers, and they were satisfied with their piece of *rus in urbe*. Over the years many of these gardens evolved into neighborhood parks that served a neighborhood constituency beyond the immediate abutters.

Although caring for the gardens has always required a great amount of attention, their stewards have, when necessary, been able to alter traditional arrangements for managing the gardens. In London, where the gardens were originally privately owned, residents of the squares relied heavily on the estate owners' willingness to fund major capital expenses. When the estate owners finally grew tired of spending money on the gardens, some of them relinquished control and either sold the property to a public agency or to the residents. Although now less exclusive, many of the gardens that have been opened to the public are still functioning as passive green spaces for the neighborhood. Meanwhile, residents' committees charged with caring for the gardens that are still private are responsible for raising enough money through assessed rates to maintain these gardens adequately. This is not always an easy task because not everyone is willing to pay his or her share.

In Boston, arrangements affecting private versus public access to, as well as maintenance of, the gardens have also changed significantly. In creating a group of garden squares for financial gain, the city of Boston acted boldly but a bit naively. By 1850, when it was ready to lay out three new squares, the city was no doubt already familiar with the high standards of landscape maintenance expected by the residents in Blackstone and Franklin squares. Yet the city was seeking short-term benefits and was not concerned with potential maintenance problems in the future. In the South End during the mid-nineteenth century, the residents of the squares soon took an active role in embellishing the gardens, but when they did, they often locked the gates and treated them as private gardens. The proprietors of Boston's Louisburg Square chose to hold on to their garden, although on many occasions some of them considered handing it over to the city. But whatever the management structure of the gardens, there has always (even in the case of Louisburg Square) been a need for cooperation and the sharing of responsibilities between the public and private sectors, because maintenance issues continue to be a great challenge for all concerned.

Because many of London's garden squares are much older than those in Boston, the appearance of the gardens has changed significantly over the years to reflect contemporary landscape styles. During the first quarter of the eighteenth century the London gardens were formal, with straight paths, geometric grass plats, and a fence, usually of brick and wood; but by the end of the century the usual design had become less formal. Trees, shrubs, and grass—still enclosed by a railing, which by then was made of iron—were laid out in a more natural, informal arrangement. Humphry Repton's 1804 plan for the ten-acre garden in Russell Square called for a clipped hornbeam hedge around the perimeter serving as a screen, and a broad gravel walk shaded by two rows of lindens encircling a grass lawn. Repton's inclusion of flower gardens and a small garden house suggests that even as early as the beginning of the nineteenth century the residents of London's squares wanted their gardens to be embellished with flowers.

Although the city of Boston designed all the South End squares to include grass, trees, and paths, only Blackstone and Franklin squares have retained their original planting designs. Even so, efforts to replicate the original tree pattern have not been very satisfactory. Blackstone Square has a dearth of trees (possibly the result of poor drainage conditions), which makes it look quite barren. The tree canopy in Franklin Square, on the other hand, is almost too dense and out of scale because more of the old trees have survived.

The early residents of Chester Square, Union Park, and Worcester Square lost no time in decorating their gardens with flowers. At the end of the twentieth century the residents were just as interested as their nineteenth-century predecessors had been in having a beautiful garden to look out on, despite the fact that the additional plantings required more care than the city was willing to provide. In Union Park the two fountains are now bordered by perennials, and the central path has been covered up. In Worcester Square the reconstructed garden includes a central path, but there is a modern fountain surrounded by rose bushes.

The gardens of the South End squares still contain a large number of character-defining features in comparison to their London counterparts. Their planting designs have already been discussed. In addition, their overall size has not changed (except for Worcester Square, which was narrowed slightly to make the streets wider, and Chester Square, which was split in half), and a few of their original furnishings remain. The original fountains have survived in Blackstone and Franklin squares. The fountains in Union Park are reproductions cast from a piece of the original fountain, but unfortunately the decorative sculptures that once enhanced these two fountains are gone. The 1913 fences, which replaced earlier makeshift fences, are still standing in Concord and Rutland squares. However, the fence in Union Park that was installed several years earlier is one foot lower than the original Louisburg Square–style fence, which makes it appear out of scale in relationship to the abutting row houses. The signature fences that now surround all of the gardens not only indicate that each garden was part of a historic square but also, in most cases, provide the abutters with a means for controlling access to these gardens.

It is important not to forget that their residential buildings have always been an integral part of garden squares. These houses have continued to serve as architectural shapers of the outdoor spaces, while their occupants have always been very involved in the management of the gardens. The South End squares are distinguished by the fact that their row houses have remained intact for almost 150 years and have never ceased to serve as residences. Today, as in the past, the residents are perhaps more interested in keeping the gardens well maintained than in understanding and acting on the range of preservation treatments available or making the most appropriate choices for these historic landscapes.

In many London squares either the original buildings are gone or, where the terrace houses remain (in Bedford Square, for example) they have been converted to offices. Without the presence of concerned residents, the use and appearance of the gardens has occasionally been affected adversely, although in some cases the estate owners have continued to keep the gardens well maintained. Even though Russell Square has lost most of its original residences, its large public garden is popular because guests from the surrounding hotels and institutions as well as many students tend to visit the garden. Given such heavy use, and perhaps also because the square has been maintained by the public sector, the garden has appeared unkempt in the past. Now that the garden has been rehabilitated, one can hope that it will benefit from a higher level of maintenance.

During the early twentieth century, Boston seriously considered upgrading the squares of the South End even though they were in an already deteriorating neighborhood. The city recommended the installation of new benches and drinking fountains so that most of the gardens could function as passive parks for the surrounding neighborhood. In all of Boston's squares except Blackstone and Franklin squares, space limitations prevented the addition of furnishings that encouraged active recreation and were not consistent with the traditional furnishings of garden squares—for instance, children's play equipment.

The addition of modern furnishings not found in the early gardens has been more common in the London squares. Many of London's gardens now contain playgrounds, tennis courts, and even bowling greens, but these features are usually camouflaged so that they do not intrude visually. These amenities not only result in a safe place for children to play but also offer opportunities for neighbors to socialize while participating in physical activities.

Only in the past few years has the city of London begun to focus on improving the 461 squares that are protected from development under the 1931 London Squares Preservation Act. As the home of so many squares—now numbering about 600—London is beginning to appreciate both the complexity and the benefits of these historic landscape treasures. The gardens in the squares are currently at different stages of the restoration process, and to date there has been more emphasis on restoring the signature railings than on deciding whether to restore other character-defining landscape features.

English Heritage's Campaign for London Squares has emphasized the present-day role of garden squares and their contribution to the human scale of the city rather than their value as a large group of unique historic landscapes that must be restored to their original appearance. Because the gardens were visible from outside their railings, even when they were all privately owned, they have always been part of the public realm for everyone to enjoy. And since London has so many squares, it is understandable that the campaign has promoted these squares as offering major social, cultural, visual, environmental, and economic benefits to the city as a whole. The South End, in contrast, is a small district with proportionately fewer squares, yet these squares also contribute to the quality of life of its residents in much the same way as London's squares do.

In her 1961 book *The Death and Life of Great American Cities*, Jane Jacobs compares the then-current condition of each of Philadelphia's four garden squares and concludes that each square's appearance is a function of the level of involvement of people in its surrounding neighborhood. Although Jacobs considers these squares large neighborhood parks and does not acknowledge their historical significance, she speaks of the importance of the "edges"—the users and occupants of the surrounding buildings—in creating a diverse constituency that will use, protect, and care for these landscapes.

Jacobs was in essence saying that of Philadelphia's four public squares only one, Rittenhouse Square, had a successful garden because its constituency was so diverse—residents who lived nearby, office workers who used the garden at lunchtime, and visitors who came to the area to shop. Rittenhouse Square, which is now a match for the best of London's squares, is the product of a very successful public/private partnership. The private sector—both residents and corporate neighbors—not only understands the economic benefits of keeping the garden well maintained but also is committed to keeping its 1913 design intact.

Gardens in the squares of London, Boston, and Philadelphia have continued to serve as focal points for their immediate neighborhoods in much the same way that Boston's more recent neighborhood parks have functioned. Neighborhood parks are currently enjoying a renaissance in Boston, where the city is committed to upgrading the smaller parks that have deteriorated from heavy use. Since these parks are all owned by the city and many are located in poor neighborhoods, supplemental funding from the private sector is rarely available. When the city improves older parks or designs new parks, it responds to input from the community during the planning stage. This participatory process, which is sometimes contentious and always time consuming, usually results in either compromise or consensus about many of the issues. The most controversial issues tend to be how much space should be allocated for active recreation—dogs, play equipment, and so forth—and for passive recreation. Only when these parks are in historic districts has there been any interest in using "acorn" lights, Victorian-style benches, and black iron fencing, which replicate furnishings used elsewhere in the district.

James Hayes Park in the South End is an interesting example of a small, contemporary neighborhood park that at first glance could be the garden of a historic square. The most obvious sign that it was not created as a centerpiece for a mid-nineteenth-century residential square is that it occupies a corner lot between West Canton Street and Warren Avenue and, therefore, does not have streets on all four sides. Hayes Park was constructed in 1993 in response to neighborhood interest in converting what was formerly a twelve-thousand-square-foot playground into a beautiful garden that everyone could enjoy. Starting in 1987, the landscape consultant provided by the Boston Redevelopment Authority worked closely with the surrounding community to develop the final design concept. Although the park includes a small area with play equipment, most of its features invite neighbors to sit and linger. Mature trees from the original playground are supplemented with flowering pear trees. Lush plantings include a circular flowerbed in the center and rose bushes that screen the play equipment. Traditional materials and furnishings—a simple black metal fence, Victorian-style benches, and a generous use of gray granite—convey the feeling that the park has been there longer than a decade.

Hayes Park has succeeded for some of the same reasons that the gardens in the South End's historic squares have survived—because of the continued and active involvement of so many neighbors. This participation translates into an extremely high level of maintenance for the park. The Friends of Hayes Park raise funds to employ a landscape contractor and arborist once a year, and through a formal agreement with the Boston Parks Department, neighbors perform most of the routine maintenance functions, such as tending the park's extensive plantings, cleaning the park, and emptying the trash receptacles. The neighbors take pride in their park not only because it is beautiful but also because it is usable and inviting. Even though the park is open to everyone during the day, including children from six local day-care centers, the city permits the community to lock the gates at night in order to discourage vandalism. Despite the fact that

Hayes Park is even smaller than Union Park's garden, its design accommodates and even encourages use.

Although the city's commitment to a participatory community process in designing or redesigning all neighborhood parks is admirable, this process is not necessarily appropriate when dealing with the restoration of the South End's garden squares—or any other historic landscape, for that matter. Stewards of historic landscapes have an obligation to make informed, objective decisions regarding preservation treatments and cannot be guided by self-interest. A recent issue involving the repair of Union Park's fence illustrates the urgent need for a South End squares conservancy.

In 1990, the residents of Union Park agreed to seek funds to replace their garden's early-twentieth-century fence with a reproduction of the original lotus-stalk fence. This treatment would have been consistent with restoring the garden to its mid-nineteenth-century appearance, for its two original fountains were in the process of being restored, and all of the original row houses in the square were still intact. When funding was not secured, the matter was dropped for ten years, until the Union Park Neighborhood Association changed course and decided to seek funds to restore the existing fence rather than replacing it. The city's Browne Fund turned down this request at the recommendation of several knowledgeable individuals as well as the Boston Preservation Alliance, which believed that this issue needed more study. Although the Browne Fund rejected the association's proposal, the city's capital fund allocated $165,000 toward the repair of the later, existing fence. This decision was based solely on the erroneous assumption that the entire neighborhood was in favor of repairing rather then replacing the fence.

The South End's garden squares represent the best of both the past and the present. They are historically important because they include landscapes that were intended to enhance the surrounding mid-nineteenth-century buildings, which in most cases are still intact. Although the gardens in Blackstone, Franklin, and Chester squares are now functioning as neighborhood parks, the public sector—the primary funding source for improvements to the gardens—must not lose sight of their historic value and treat them simply as neighborhood parks. Also, it is essential that the private stewards of all the gardens understand their historical significance and attempt to educate others, including the public sector, about their value. A private South End squares conservancy could work with the city's Parks Department to prepare a comprehensive restoration plan for the gardens in all of the eight South End squares. To be most effective this plan should focus on the gardens collectively as well as individually. Without a local advocacy organization promoting the interests of all the squares as members of a family of historic landscapes and insisting on the appropriate preservation treatment for the garden in each one of them, the original integrity of the South End's garden squares will begin to erode.

Bibliography

The discussion of garden squares as presented in this book encompasses several disciplines—landscape design, architecture, social and economic history, and preservation—within the context of different cities. Books and articles in the bibliography are divided into sections according to the primary city they describe, specifically, Boston, London, and Other U.S. Cities. There also is a section for Records.

BOSTON

Bacon's Dictionary of Boston. Historical intro. by George E. Ellis. Boston: Houghton Mifflin, 1886.

Barrows, Esther G. *Neighbors All: A Settlement Notebook.* Boston: Houghton Mifflin, 1929.

The Boston Almanac for the Year 1852. Boston: B. B. Muss & Co., 1852.

Boston Redevelopment Authority. *South End/Lower Roxbury Development Policy Plan: A Plan to Encourage and Guide Growth,* 1993.

Brown, Frank Chouteau. "The First Residential 'Row Houses' in Boston." *Old-Time New England* 37, no. 3 (January 1947): 60–69.

Campbell, Robert. "Federal Appeal." *The Boston Globe Magazine.* September 15, 1996: 20–30.

Card, Richard O. "Twenty-Five Years of Leadership: The South End Historical Society, Inc." *The SEHS Newsletter* 20, no. 2 (Spring 1991).

Chamberlain, Allen. *Beacon Hill: Its Ancient Pastures and Early Mansions.* Boston: Houghton Mifflin, 1925.

Dwight, Timothy. *Travels in New England and New York.* Ed. by Barbara Miller Solomon. Vol. 4. Cambridge, Mass.: Belknap Press of Harvard University Press, 1969.

Farquhar, Anna (Margaret Allston). *Her Boston Experiences: A Picture of Modern Boston Society and People.* Illus. by Frank O. Small. Boston: L. C. Page & Co., 1900.

Goldberg, Carey. "Behind the Curtains of Boston's Best Neighborhood, a New York Elite." *New York Times.* February 18, 1999: A16.

Holleran, Michael. *Boston's "Changeful Times": Origins of Preservation and Planning in America.* Baltimore: Johns Hopkins University Press, 1998.

Janes, Kirtland, & Co. *Ornamental Ironwork.* Reprint of 1870 illustrated catalog. Princeton: Pyne Press, 1971.

Kennedy, Albert J. "The South End." *Our Boston* 2, no. 1 (Dec. 1926): 13–19.

Kennedy, Lawrence W. *Planning the City upon a Hill: Boston Since 1630.* Amherst: University of Massachusetts Press, 1992.

Kirker, Harold. *The Architecture of Charles Bulfinch.* Cambridge, Mass.: Harvard University Press, 1969.

Kirker, Harold and James. *Bulfinch's Boston.* New York: Oxford University Press, 1964.

The Life and Letters of Charles Bulfinch, Architect: With Other Family Papers. Ed. by Ellen Susan Bulfinch. Intro. by Charles A. Cummings. Boston: Houghton Mifflin, 1896.

Lukas, J. Anthony. *Common Ground: A Turbulent Decade in the Lives of Three American Families.* New York: Alfred A. Knopf, 1985.

Lynch, Kevin. *The Image of the City.* Cambridge, Mass.: M.I.T. Press, 1960.

Mapping Boston. Ed. by Alex Krieger and David Cobb with Amy Turner. Cambridge, Mass.: M.I.T. Press, 1999.

Moore, Barbara W., and Gail Weesner. *Beacon Hill: A Living Portrait.* Boston: Centry Hill Press, 1992.

Nylander, Jane. "Henry Sargent's Dinner and Tea Party." *Antiques* (May 1982): 1171–1183.

Pemberton, Thomas. "A Topographical and Historical Description of Boston." *Collections of the Massachusetts Historical Society* 3 (1794): 241–304.

Place, Charles, A. *Charles Bulfinch: Architect and Citizen.* New York: Da Capo Press, 1968.

Shurtleff, Nathaniel B. *A Topographical and Historical Description of Boston.* 3rd ed. Boston: Rockwell and Churchill, City Printers, 1891.

Smith, Margaret Supplee. "Between City and Suburb: Architecture and Planning in Boston's South End." Ph.D. diss. Brown University, 1976.

————, and John C. Moorhouse. "Architecture and the Housing Market: Nineteenth Century Row Housing in Boston's South End." *Journal of the Society of Architectural Historians* 52, no. 2 (June 1993): 159–178.

Southworth, Susan and Michael. *Ornamental Ironwork: An Illustrated Guide to Its Design, History and Use in American Architecture.* Boston: David R. Godine, 1978.

Von Hoffman, Alexander. *Local Attachments: The Making of an American Urban Neighborhood, 1850–1920.* Baltimore: Johns Hopkins University Press, 1986.

Waite, Emma Forbes. "The Tontine Crescent and Its Architect." *Old-Time New England* 43, no. 3 (Winter 1953): 74–77.

Warner, Sam B., Jr. *The Streetcar Suburbs: The Process of Growth in Boston, 1870–1900.* New York: Atheneum, 1973.

Weinhardt, Carl J., Jr. "The Domestic Architecture of Beacon Hill, 1800–1850." Rpt. from *Proceedings of the Bostonian Society*, Annual Meeting, 1958. Boston: Bostonian Society, 1973.

Whitehill, Walter Muir. "The Metamorphosis of Scollay and Bowdoin Squares." Rpt. from the *Proceedings of the Bostonian Society*, Annual Meetings, 1972–1973. Boston: Bostonian Society, 1973.

————. *Boston: A Topographical History*. Cambridge, Mass.: Belknap Press of Harvard University Press, 1959.

Willard, Ashton R. "Charles Bulfinch, the Architect." *The New England Magazine* 3, no. 3 (November 1890): 272–299.

Winkley, Hobart W. "Annals of Louisburgh Square 1920." Unpublished manuscript at the Boston Athenaeum, Boston, Mass.

Wolfe, Albert Benedict. *The Lodging-House Problem in Boston*. Boston: Houghton Mifflin, 1906.

Wood, Joseph S. *The New England Village*. Baltimore: Johns Hopkins University Press, 1997.

Woods, Robert A., ed. *The City Wilderness: A Settlement Study by Residents and Associates of the South End House*. Boston: Houghton Mifflin, 1898.

LONDON

Byrne, Andrew. *Bedford Square: An Architectural Study*. London: Athlone Press, 1990.

A Campaign for London Squares. London: English Heritage, 2002.

Chancellor, E. Beresford. *The History of the Squares of London: Topographical and Historical*. London: Kegan Paul, Trench, Trubner & Co., 1907.

Cruickshank, Dan, and Neil Burton. *Life in the Georgian City*. London: Viking, 1990.

Davis, John P. S. *Antique Garden Ornament: 300 Years of Creativity: Artists, Manufacturers & Materials*. Woodbridge, Suffolk, Eng.: Antique Collectors' Club, 1991.

Forrest, Denys. *St. James's Square: People, Houses, Happenings*. London: Quiller Press, 1986.

Forshaw, Alec, and Theo Bergström. *The Open Spaces of London*. London: Allison and Busby, 1986.

Girouard, Mark. *The English Town: A History of Urban Life*. New Haven and London: Yale University Press, 1990.

Gwynn, John. *London and Westminster Improved*. Illustrated by plans. London, 1766.

Hibbert, Christopher. *London: The Biography of a City*. London: Penguin Books, 1983.

Jones, Edward, and Christopher Woodward. *A Guide to the Architecture of London*. 2nd ed. New York: Thames and Hudson, 1992.

London Squares. The Proceedings of the London Squares Conference, "A Forum on the Past, Present and Future of London's Squares." June 26, 1995. London: London Historic Parks and Gardens Trust, 1997.

Longstaff-Gowan, Todd. *The London Town Garden 1700–1840*. New Haven and London: Yale University Press, 2001.

Olsen, Donald J. *Town Planning in London: The Eighteenth and Nineteenth Centuries*. New Haven and London: Yale University Press, 1964.

Rasmussen, Steen Eiler. *London: The Unique City*. Rev. ed. Cambridge, Mass.: M.I.T. Press, 1982.

Report of the Royal Commission on London Squares. London: His Majesty's Stationery Office, 1928.

Stuart, James. *Critical Observations on the Buildings and Improvements of London*. London: J. Dodsley, 1771.

Summerson, John. *Georgian London*. 3rd ed. Cambridge, Mass.: M.I.T. Press, 1978.

Tames, Richard. *Bloomsbury Past: A Visual History*. London: Historical Publications Ltd., 1993.

OTHER U.S. CITIES

Dorsey, John. *Mount Vernon Place: An Anecdotal Essay with 66 Illustrations*. Baltimore: Maclay & Associates, 1983.

Downing, Andrew Jackson. *Rural Essays*. Ed. by George William Curtis. New York: Da Capo Press, 1974.

Garmey, Stephen. *Gramercy Park: An Illustrated History of a New York Neighborhood*. Foreword by Paul Goldberger. N.p.: Balsam Press, 1984.

Hayward, Mary Ellen, and Charles Belfoure. *The Baltimore Rowhouse*. Foreword by James Marston Fitch. New York: Princeton Architectural Press, 1999.

Jacobs, Jane. *The Death and Life of Great American Cities*. New York: Random House, 1961.

Lane, Mills. *Savannah Revisited: History & Architecture*. Savannah: Beehive Press, 1994.

Lockwood, Charles. *Bricks & Brownstone: The New York Row House, 1783–1929: An Architectural & Social History*. Intro. by James Biddle. New York: McGraw-Hill, 1972.

———. *Manhattan Moves Uptown: An Illustrated History*. Boston: Houghton Mifflin, 1976.

Murtagh, William John. "The Philadelphia Row House." *Journal of the Society of Architectural Historians* 16, no. 4 (Dec. 1957).

Reps, John W. *The Making of Urban America: A History of City Planning in the United States*. Princeton: Princeton University Press, 1965.

Scharf, J. Thomas, and Thompson Westcott. *History of Philadelphia 1609–1884*. Vol. 3. Philadelphia: L. H. Everts and Co., 1884.

Schuyler, David. *The New Urban Landscape: The Redefinition of City Form in Nineteenth-Century America*. Baltimore: Johns Hopkins University Press, 1986.

The Secretary of the Interior's Standards for the Treatment of Historic Properties: With Guidelines for the Treatment of Cultural Landscapes. Ed. by Charles A. Birnbaum with Christine Capella Peters. Washington, D.C.: U.S. Department of the Interior, National Park Service, 1996.

Sieg, Chan. *The Squares: An Introduction to Savannah*. Norfolk, Va.: Donning Co., 1984.

Thompson, D. G. Brinton. *Ruggles of New York: A Life of Samuel B. Ruggles*. New York: Columbia University Press, 1946.

Trollope, Frances. *Domestic Manners of the Americans*. Ed. by Donald Smalley. New York: Alfred A. Knopf, 1949.

Webb, Michael. *The City Square: A Historical Evolution*. London: Thames and Hudson, 1990.

RECORDS

Boston City Directory, 1826–1860. Boston Public Library.

Boston City Documents, 1822–1863 and 1879–1914. Boston Public Library.

Olmsted Archives. Frederick Law Olmsted National Historic Site, Brookline, Mass. Olmsted Job #950, Public Grounds Dept./City Squares, Boston, Mass.

Olmsted Papers. Library of Congress, Washington, D.C. Correspondence for Job #950, 1911–1915.

Proprietors of Louisburg Square. *Records, 1826–1980.* Massachusetts Historical Society. Boston, Mass.

A Record of the Streets, Alleys, Places, Etc., in the City of Boston. Boston: City of Boston, 1902.

"Report of the Special Committee of the Parkman Fund Income." *Boston City Document* 103. 1921.

Suffolk County Deeds, 1795–1850. Edward W. Brooke Courthouse. Boston, Mass.

Index

Page numbers in *italics* refer to illustrations.

Briggs, Luther, Jr., 92
Brown, Lancelot "Capability," 7
Browne Fund. *See* Edward Ingersoll
  Browne Fund
brownstone construction: Back Bay,
  118; Blackstone and Franklin
  squares, 79–80, 82, 83, *83, 86*;
  Chester Square, 90; New York
  City row houses, 16; Union Park,
  101
Bryant, Gridley J. F., 104
Buckingham, James Silk, 14
builders vs. architects as designers of
  row houses, xv, 31, 42, 92–93
building construction: garden squares
  as incentive for, 82; materials for
  New York City row houses, 16;
  restrictions on, 59, 69, 115; South
  End issues with, 75, 77; stone
  construction, 42, 69; stucco, 30.
  See also brick construction; brownstone construction
buildings, as focus of town squares,
  xii. *See also* attached houses
Bulfinch, Charles: as creator of Boston
  squares, 18–19; financial risk taken
  by, 64; Franklin Place project, xi,
  25–39; London inspiration for, xv;
  and Louisburg Square, 40–41; and
  Mount Vernon Proprietors, 39;
  and Philadelphia squares, 10;
  vision for South End, 68–72
burial grounds, squares as, 11
buses. *See* omnibuses
business owners, as residents of downtown squares, 62

Campbell, Colin, 5
Canby brothers, 17
Carlton Park, Boston, 112
Carnes, William, 90, 94
Carpenter, William, 92
carriageways, 7
cast iron, use of, 42, 80, 82, *91*, 143.
  See also fencing; fountains
Cathedral Housing Project, Boston,
  137
cattle pastures, squares as, 11, 14
Center Plaza, Boston, 63, *63*
Center Square, Philadelphia, 10, 11
Central Park, New York City, 16
Charles I (King of England), 1
Chester Square, Boston: decline of,
  132, 133–34; development of, 75,

82, 86–97, *87, 89, 91, 93, 95, 96,
  122*; location, *66*; and revival
  of South End, 137; size of, 20;
  twentieth-century improvements,
  123–24, 126–28, 135, 145–48, *147*;
  vs. Union Park, 103
Chickering, Jonas, 84
children, and pressure to improve
  South End squares, 131
Chilson, Gardner, 78, 80
Church of the Immaculate Conception, Boston, 78
churches, as garden square attractions,
  2, 26, 35, 37, 78, 84
City Wilderness, The (Woods), 121
classes, social. *See individual classes*
Cochituate Water Works, 43–44, 90
Collington Square, Baltimore, 18
Colonnade, the, Boston, 25
Columbia Square, Boston, 19, 68–69,
  70–72
commercialization of squares: and
  downtown Boston, 23, 35, 56;
  for lodging house residents, 132;
  in London, 2, 150, 155; in New
  York City, 16, 38–39; in South
  End, 57, 61, 62–63, 117
commons, town, xi, 1
Commonwealth Avenue, Boston, 118
Complete Body of Architecture, A
  (Ware), 5–6
Concord Square, Boston: development of, 110–12; location, *66*;
  twentieth-century improvements,
  125, 128–29, 146, *147*
conservancy, need for in South End,
  157–58, 165–66
construction. *See* building construction
Cooper, Peter, 10–11
Copley, John Singleton, 39, 57
cotton industry, and growth of Savannah, 13–14
Cotton (Pemberton) Hill, Boston,
  24, 57
Covent Garden Piazza, London, 2
crescent layout for garden squares,
  18–20, 27, 29, 57–58, 63
*Critical Observations on the Buildings and
  Improvements of London* (Stuart), 7

Dearborn, Axel, 90
*Death and Life of Great American Cities,
  The* (Jacobs), 163

developers: and Baltimore squares, 17;
  and downtown Boston squares,
  23–24, 56, 57; and financial incentives for garden squares, xii, xiv;
  London vs. Boston development
  of squares, 1–2, 113–16; and New
  York City residential development, 16, 37; and Philadelphia
  squares, 11; role in American
  square development, 10, 15; and
  Savannah squares, 14; and vari-
  ations in town house design, 5.
  See also estate owners, London;
  speculative building
Dexter, George Minot, 59, *59*, 60, 62
Dinner Party, The (Sargent), 33, 34
Domestic Manners of the Americans
  (Trollope), 11, 38
double houses, for Franklin Place,
  29–30
Downing, Andrew Jackson, xi
downtown garden squares, Boston:
  brick construction, 42; commercialization of, 23, 35, 56; financial
  rewards of, 19; historical context,
  24–25; map, *22*; overview, 23–24;
  Pemberton Square, 19, *22*, 23, 56–
  65, *60, 61, 62, 63*; vs. South End,
  20, 67–68; ultimate demise of, 64–
  65. *See also* Franklin Place, Boston;
  Louisburg Square, Boston
drinking fountains, introduction of,
  124, 126–27, 131
Druid Hill Park, Baltimore, 18
Dwight, Timothy, xi–xii

economics: Baltimore city growth, 17;
  cyclical effects on South End, 118–
  19; and garden square creation, 9;
  London vs. Boston squares, 64–65;
  manufacturing effects on South
  End, 72, 94, 119, 131; revival of
  South End, 137. *See also* commercialization of squares; financing of
  garden improvements
Edward Ingersoll Browne Fund, 138,
  143, 146
elevated railway, intrusion into South
  End, 119, 128, *129*, 137
elm trees: Blackstone Square, 81,
  125–26; Chester Square, *87*, 127;
  Concord Square, 128–29; Franklin
  Place, *36*; Franklin Square, Boston,
  79, 125–26, *130*; Louisburg Square,

Neck, the, Boston, 69–70, 73. *See also* South End district, Boston

neighborhood parks, renaissance of in Boston, 163–64

Neighbors All (Barrows), 121

neoclassical style, 5, 25, 27–29, 28, 34

New York City: brownstones in, 84; garden square development in, 15, 15–16; Gramercy Park, 55–56; London influence on squares, 10; patterns of square development, 18; St. John's Park, 16, 35, 37–39

Newton, William, 1–2

Nichols, Sutton, 3, 4, 6

Northeast (Franklin) Square, Philadelphia, 12

Oglethorpe, James, 12–13

Olmsted, Frederick Law, Sr., 130

Olmsted Brothers firm, 124, 126

omnibuses, 72, 86

ornamentation, 5, 80, 82, 93, 101

Otis, Harrison Gray, 40–41

ownership of garden squares, private vs. public: American traditions, 10; in Baltimore, 17–18; downtown vs. South End, 67–68; Franklin Place, 32; in London, 1, 54–55; London vs. Boston, 113–16, 160; Louisburg Square, 41, 44, 49; in New York City, 16; overview of Boston issues, 19, 20, 21; partnership between, 80, 134, 140–50, 163; unresolved issues over, 151–52, 156. *See also* developers; public amenities, squares as; residents

Palladian style, 2, 5–6, 9

Palladio, Andrea, 5

park furnishings: Franklin Square, Boston, 129, 130; lighting fixtures, 59, 135, 145, 146; in London squares, 162–63; and twentieth-century improvements, 123–24, 131–32, 134–35, 138

Park Row, Boston, 25

parking, in garden squares, 6, 54, 55

Parkman, George F., 123

parks, xi, xiii, 14, 163–64. *See also individual parks*

pastoral landscape style, 7

paths/walkways, 6, 14, 17, 88–89

Pemberton, Thomas, 32

Pemberton (Cotton) Hill, Boston, 24, 57

Pemberton Square, Boston: development of, 19, 23, 56–65, 60, 61, 62, 63; location, 22

Penn, William, 10

Pepperrell, William (Sir), 40

Perkins, James, 33

Perkins, Thomas Handasyd, Jr., 42

Perkins Square, Baltimore, 17–18

Philadelphia garden squares, 9–12, 14, 163

poor classes, in South End, 103–4, 118, 119, 136

port towns, as focus of garden squares, xi

Practice of Architecture, The (Benjamin), 41

preservation: Louisburg Square, 49; need for guidelines on, 143; residents' concerns with, xiv, 21, 162; and stewardship of South End, 140–50; strategies for South End, 155–58. *See also* maintenance and preservation

privacy: Chester Square, 96; Hayes Park, 164–65; and interior gardens, 112–13; and locked garden squares, 8, 148; London squares, 2, 53, 151–52, 155; Louisburg Square, 43, 49; modern need for limited access, 138, 142; residents' interest in, 9; of streets in garden squares, xiii, 19, 59, 103. *See also* fencing

promenading, 6, 85

property owners, as maintainers of gardens, 77, 103, 136. *See also* developers; estate owners, London; residents

Prudential Center, Boston, 135

public amenities, squares as: in Baltimore, 17–18; and cost of development, 113; and financial incentives for garden squares, 68, 74, 86–87; in London, 54, 150–55, 163–64; maintenance and preservation challenges, 14, 51–52, 76–77, 96, 100, 106, 108; need for Boston city leadership, 156–58; in New York City, 16, 55; in Savannah, 10, 14; social role of, 84–86, 131. *See also* maintenance and preservation; ownership of garden squares,

private vs. public; South End district, Boston

purchasers. *See* developers; property owners as maintainers of gardens; residents

Quattro Libri (Palladio), 5

Quincy, Josiah, 69

railroads, development of, 72, 119

real estate values. *See* value, real estate

reconstruction of historic landscapes, vs. other treatments, 156

recreation, passive vs. active, 17, 149–50, 164

rehabilitation of historic landscapes, vs. other treatments, 153, 156

Repton, Humphry, 7, 153, 160

residential squares. *See* garden squares

residents: and leasehold arrangement, 3; as maintainers of gardens, 43, 45, 51–56, 58–59, 77, 111, 138, 141–42; as owners of gardens, 37–38; preservation concerns, xiv, 21, 162; and private vs. public ownership of squares, 137, 151–52; real estate value concerns, 140; and social functions of gardens, 71, 149, 163; as stewards of gardens, xiii, 21, 96–97, 115, 134, 135. *See also individual social classes*

restoration: for Blackstone and Franklin squares, 144; as challenge for middle-class residents, 135; in London squares, 162–63; vs. other treatments for historic landscapes, 143, 153, 156, 157; as South End focus, 155–56

Rise of Silas Lapham, The (Howells), 117

Rittenhouse Square, Philadelphia, 12, 163

Rogers, Charles O., 92

rooming-house district, South End as, 120–21

row houses: as addition to elite mansions in town, 40; in Back Bay, 118; in Baltimore, 17, 18; Berwick Park, 111–12; Blackstone and Franklin squares, 77, 82–84; builders vs. architects as designers of, xv, 31, 42, 92–93; Bulfinch-designed, 25–39; Columbia Square, 70; consistent preservation of, 149; continued

PHEBE S. GOODMAN is a landscape designer with a special interest in urban parks. For many years she served as executive director of the Friends of Copley Square, which works in partnership with the Boston Parks and Recreation Department to maintain Copley Square. She worked as a landscape preservation consultant for the Chester Square Neighborhood Association in Boston's South End during their planning for possible reconstruction of the garden. Between 1997 and 2002 she was also president of the Shirley-Eustis House Association, stewards of a 1747 royal governor's mansion in the Roxbury neighborhood of Boston.